Food Truckin'

Recipes from the World's Best Food Trucks

Published in 2015 by Graffito Books Ltd.,
32 Great Sutton Street,
London EC1V 0NB
www.graffitobooks.com

Editor: Katriona Feinstein
Art Direction: Karen Wilks
Recipe Editor: Serena Pethick

British Library cataloguing-in-publication data:
A catalogue record of this book is available at The British Library.

Printed in China.

Food Truckin'

Recipes from the World's Best Food Trucks

GRAFFITO

Contents

LEFT: Truck as art - the amazing Del Popolo Food Truck from San Francisco.

Introduction

People love food trucks because they redefine the way we eat, how we eat and the places we eat in. There's a feeling of adventurous whim with a food truck experience because of the hunter-gatherer nature of it. The truck is always moving around, and so the meal has to be worked for – the truck is not just delivering a fusion taco then, but a prize. This gives the eater a kind of status in the food world – a cool factor.

Food truck food has also become, by definition, more of an adventurous cuisine: a place where technique, ingredients and cultural references have become extremely playful and reinvented. It has an addictive quality. And, because of the lower barrier of entry to start a food truck, there is a more youthful, creative and experimental quality to food truck signature dishes. A traditional restaurant often needs to play it safer in order to recruit a more mainstream audience.

Although street food has ancient roots – often with a mobile component – the US put an original, modern spin on things in the last decade that has now spread throughout the world. This global food truck movement truly would not have been so without our social media-crazy zeitgeist. Trucks like ours use geo-based tweets to disclose locations and up-to-the-minute menu updates; but consumers have also showcased trucks online, updating their statuses to show they are cool enough to hunt them down, disclosing their menu selections and interacting with the truck owners about their experiences. The food truck movement needed these open and very visual networks. It is the combination of the social media online element, the fusion food, and the can-do, pro-business attitude in post-recession times that has been America's influence on the food truck movement. It is what has defined this era of street food.

As the industry has matured, the opportunity has emerged for small, independent trucks to blow up and become nationwide brands. Coolhaus is a case in point. We started off as two young women with a tiny ice cream truck; we now have a national fleet, two brick-and-mortars in L.A., and a burgeoning distribution business. What I have always loved about food trucking remains unchanged – no two days are ever the same. That can be good and bad, of course. We could be doing sponsored giveaways in Times Square, having a great day at Coachella Music Festival, or watching a couple propose at our truck. Or our truck could be breaking down in Malibu with no reception, our freezer could stop working in the middle of a service, or a heated territory war might ensue on a crowded street. I have come to love the unpredictability! It keeps you on your toes. While the food truck industry will continue to grow, this spontaneity will stay the same. You never know exactly what you're going to get – whether it's a Korean-Mexican taco from L.A. or a Vietnamese-Peruvian salad from Melbourne. That's what this book is all about: discovering and re-creating delicious, unlikely treats from all corners of the food truck world.

- Natasha Case, Co-founder Coolhaus, Los Angeles.

LEFT: One of the Coolhaus Trucks in California.

Engine

Engine is recognized as one of London's outstanding food trucks. Owner Richard Shanks, however, hadn't always intended a career in street food. "After training as an actor, it became very apparent that I was going to need another income stream." His food truck career began with The Little Mixing Factory, Britain's first frozen yogurt truck, which he parked up next to the River Thames. A little later, he invested in a bright red vintage Citroën H van - a retired 1959 French fire engine, from which he started to serve British chorizo, halloumi and smoked sausages. "This is where the hot dog addiction started!" He decided to narrow down his critically-acclaimed menu. "Hot Dogs in the UK have always been quite a 'budget affair', and we wanted to change that. Why not use good quality meat? Why not use an artisan bun and homemade toppings? So we did, and Engine Hot Dogs was born." He says the secret to a good dog is a moist bun that is not too bulky; his favorite is The Big Richard with homemade chipotle hot sauce. For Richard food trucks are a big success because "it is what it is. No bull. Just good people selling good food, to good people who want to eat good food. Food makes us happy. Someone should have thought of this years ago."

YOSHI DOG (JAPAN-STYLE BEEF DOG)
serves: as many as you like

Dog: We use double-smoked all-beef sausages handmade with natural casings. They're big and juicy, with the perfect snap.

Bun: We use Jewish Challah bread rolls. Made with vegetable oil, they are light, but moist, and even better when steamed. Our tip is to keep the rolls quite slim. Remember, the bun is just a carrier, the dog is the main event!

Takoyaki Sauce: Shop bought!

Crispy onions: Cheat and buy these in a packet, or try making them yourself.

Wasabi Mayo: Add wasabi to regular mayo from a jar. Start with 1 tbsp wasabi powder (NOT paste). Slowly add water to make a runny green sauce. This will blend easily with the mayo.

Seaweed: Buy sheets of Nori (typically used for Sushi) and slice finely.

Assembly: Heat your dogs in water and then finish on the grill – this will draw some of the salt and water out of the sausage. Insert into steamed bun. Apply a generous zigzag of Takoyaki sauce the whole length of the sausage. Sprinkle on a handful of crispy onions. Apply a not-quite-so generous zigzag of wasabi mayo and sprinkle with chopped seaweed to finish.
Et voilà!

GIOVANNI'S

If you happen to be on the North Shore of Oahu, Hawaii and feeling hungry, it is likely that you will be pointed to Giovanni's shrimp truck; it is the oldest and best known on the island. Giovanni's was set up in the early '90s, long before the global food truck movement got going. The Nitsche family, who run the truck, pride themselves on selling top quality, classic shrimp dishes, with a simple menu of hot and spicy shrimp, shrimp scampi and lemon butter shrimp. Although the original 1953 bread truck that Giovanni's operated from has since been upgraded, there is a certain tradition of truck decoration that the team has stuck with. In 1993, after Giovanni's truck had closed up for the night, Ed Hernandez from El Paso, TX, decided he wanted to leave his mark on the vehicle. Next morning, the truck's employees noticed the signature and decided to leave it there. The following day a few more signatures with pictures appeared and there started a tradition: thousands of customers have now signed Giovanni's truck. The Nitsches have now purchased the land the truck sits on. "All we want is for our patrons to enjoy our shrimp, the weather and each other. We will be proud to serve you for the next 20 years and beyond!"

LEMON BUTTER SHRIMP
serves: 4-6

- 2 lb (900 g) large shrimp, peeled and deveined • ½ cup butter • ¼ cup lemon juice
- 1 tsp parsley flakes • 1 tsp Worcestershire sauce
- 1 tsp soy sauce • ½ tsp salt • ½ tsp black pepper, coarsely ground • ¼ tsp garlic salt
- 1 clove garlic, minced • 2 lemons, cut into wedges • hot cooked rice

Method: On medium heat melt butter in large skillet or wok. Add next 8 ingredients and allow them to sizzle briefly. Turn heat to medium-high and add shrimp; cook for 5-7 minutes stirring occasionally. Serve over hot rice. Garnish with lemon wedges.

Burger Theory

Adelaide's Rob Dean, 29, and Canadian-born Dan Mendelson, 25, think about burgers a lot and spend a lot of time making them too. Dan was reading Sociology at Adelaide's Flinders University (his thesis: the sociology of food) when he met Rob in a Social Theory class. They talked about the street food revolution taking over the US, where all of the hottest new chefs were serving on four wheels. Adelaide it suddenly seemed, with its low-rent pie carts and chip stands, had been missing a serious trick. Rob turned down a lucrative offer to work for the London Olympics and, in 2011, the two new friends hurriedly secured truck drivers' licenses and put down $11,500 for a retired film industry catering truck. They developed a menu of 100% Coorong Angus beef burgers, with delicious gourmet touches like crispy pancetta, onion confit and Adelaide Blue cheese sauce. They call it "Thoughtful Fast Food" and their menu – which usually sells out in a couple of hours – hasn't changed much since. Since becoming Adelaide's first roaming food truck, Burger Theory has helped to change city council laws and has paved the way for Adelaide to enter the world food truck revolution. "Flat tyres aside, it's been one hell of a ride."

#1 CLASSIC BURGER
serves: 6

"An exercise in classic burger simplicity. There's iceberg lettuce for freshness and crunch, field tomatoes for acidity, sweetness and umami, American (aka processed) cheese for its unrivalled gooey texture, and truck sauce, which provides the lavish consistency only a mayonnaise can provide."

The beef: Freshly grind 2 lb (900g) of high quality chuck steak, 5 oz (150g) per burger. Do not, we repeat, DO NOT season the beef at this stage. (This is how sausage is made. Proper American burgers are always seasoned right before they hit the grill.) Form into loose patties just over ½ inch (1.5cm) thick, season both sides with fine sea salt, and cook to your desired doneness in a ripping hot cast iron pan. Put a slice of cheese on top with about a minute to go.

The toppings: Have these ready and waiting.
Truck sauce: Start with mayonnaise and add your favorite condiments; try not to let any single condiment dominate.

Assembly: Toast bun, apply truck sauce to both top and bottom bun, add a couple slices of tomatoes, place the just-cooked burger with melted cheese, crack freshly ground pepper, place a few leaves of iceberg and top with... the top bun.
Serve immediately!

BUSKRUID

If you go to Amsterdam, it will be hard to miss the shiny red fire truck from which Jessica Shrier, founder of Buskruid, prepares and serves her tasty soups and salads. In business for just two years she has already received critical acclaim - winning Best Main Dish at the British Street Food Awards - as well as achieving the status of a Must Visit Truck with food truck fans globally. Wanting to cook and travel, a food truck was a logical progression. She found her old German fire truck online and roped in her brother-in-law to help transform it into the charming eatery it is today. Jessica works with fresh, seasonal and local produce. "The soups and salads I serve are all vegetarian, to make people aware of how delicious and wholesome meatless meals can actually be." Jessica's cooking has lived up to the name 'Buskruid' (a play on the Dutch for gunpowder (buskruit) and herbs (kruid)); the locals tells us that the food is electrifying.

RED BEETROOT SOUP WITH SWEET POTATO AND HORSERADISH
serves: 6

• 1 large red onion, diced • 1 clove garlic • 2 lb 2 oz (1kg) red beetroots, finely diced
• 9 oz (250g) sweet potato • balsamic vinegar • brown sugar • virgin olive oil
• horseradish cream • fresh dill • salt & pepper

Method: Prepare horseradish cream the day before (see page 113).
Peel the beetroots, dice and rinse off.
Fry the onion and garlic for a few minutes until softened and add the beetroots and water till just covering the beets. Bring to the boil and simmer until tender. While the beets are cooking prepare the rest. Peel the sweet potato and dice (about ¼ inch [0.5cm] cubes). Boil them for 10-15 minutes until 'al dente'. Whiz the beets with a hand-held blender until smooth, (add extra water if it's too thick) then add sweet potato and a (big) splash of balsamic vinegar and a spoon of brown sugar.
Bring just back to the boil, then turn off the heat.
Season with salt and freshly ground black pepper.
Serve the soup with a small spoon of the horseradish cream and garnish with freshly chopped dill and some pepper.

'Eet smakelijk!'

COOLHAUS

Founders Natasha Case and her girlfriend Freya Estreller started baking cookies and making ice cream in 2008. With mutual backgrounds in design and real estate, they began naming their ice cream sandwiches after architects and architectural movements – and decided to take their new found passion (dubbed "Farchitecture," Food + Architecture) to their hometown streets in Los Angeles. So, after a few days cruising Craigslist, they found and bought a beat-up old postal van, trekked out to the Coachella Valley Music Festival to make their debut, and, well.... the rest is history. Coolhaus now operates a national fleet of 11 mobile ice cream trucks and carts (five in SoCal, three in NYC, two in Austin, and one in Dallas). Fans can also visit Coolhaus at its two storefronts in Culver City and Pasadena, or pick up a pre-packaged ice cream sandwich, pint of ice cream, or hand-dipped ice cream bar at one of 1,500+ gourmet markets in over 40 states.

DIRTY MINT CHIP ICE CREAM
makes: 2 quarts (1.9 litres)

"We have news for you. That supermarket mint chip ice cream with the nuclear-green color? It doesn't have any mint leaves in it. It has mint oil or fake mint flavoring. Real, fresh mint leaves give our Dirty Mint a fresh, cool intensity."

Plain Custard Base – makes 2 quarts
• 2 cups whole milk • 2 cups heavy cream • 4 cups light brown or granulated sugar • 8 egg yolks, large (as fresh as possible)

Method: In a 4-quart (4 L) saucepan, combine milk, cream and half of sugar. Set over high heat and cook, stirring occasionally, until mixture comes to a boil. Meanwhile, in a medium bowl, whisk yolks and remaining sugar until smooth, heavy and pale yellow, about 30 seconds. When cream mixture just comes to a boil, whisk, remove from heat, and, in a slow stream, pour half of the cream mixture over yolk-sugar mixture, whisking constantly until blended. Return pan to stovetop over low heat. Whisking constantly, stream yolk-cream mixture back into pan. With a wooden spoon, continue stirring until mixture registers 165°F to 180°F (75°C to 82°C) on an instant-read thermometer, about 2 minutes. Do not heat above 180°F (82°C), or eggs will scramble. The mixture should be slightly thickened and coat back of spoon, with steam rising, but not boiling. (If you blow on the back of the spoon and the mixture ripples, you've got the right consistency.) Pour base into a clean airtight container and refrigerate for at least 12 hours or 24 hours for best results. Use base within 3 to 5 days.

• ⅓ cup finely chopped fresh mint leaves • ½ tbsp dark brown sugar • ¼ tsp kosher salt • 2 quarts (1.9 litres) plain custard base, made with light brown sugar instead of granulated • ½ cup mini semisweet chocolate chips

Method: Stir mint leaves, dark brown sugar and salt into custard base. Mix well. Process in an ice cream-maker according to manufacturer's instructions. Transfer to a bowl and fold in chocolate chips. Scrape into an airtight storage container. Freeze for a minimum of 2 hours before serving.

The Good Life

There are few food truck locations more idyllic than the iconic Twelve Apostles mountain range in Cape Town. Chef, founder and marketeer extraordinaire, Adele Maartens, regularly leaves the bustle of the city and takes her truck up to the mountains to serve great food to tourists and walkers. "It is absolutely beautiful. They buy their lunch from us, sit on the rocks and enjoy their food with the fresh breeze in their hair." Adele has sought inspiration from travels in Morocco, Thailand and Holland to create her unique exotic menu of fresh fusion food. At any one time her menu might consist of prawn tempura with sumac aioli, designer beef burgers with a truffle infusion, venison burgers with bourbon-poached pears and brie, Thai crab salad wrap, or Moroccan chicken with vegetable couscous pitta. She believes it is the variety of her menu, as well as her organic ingredients and high-end flavour combinations, that make The Good Life the firm favourite that it is in the Cape. Not always situated in the mountains, Adele also likes to make her presence known in Oudekraal in front of Charly's bakery on Harrington Street.

CHEESE BURGER WITH JACK DANIELS ONION RELISH
makes: 6 burgers

Burgers: • 6 burger buns • cheese • tomatoes • rocket
Patties: • 1 lb 12 oz (800g) minced beef • 1 chopped onion • ½ cup flat leaf parsley • 1 egg yolk • 1 clove garlic, diced • 1 tbsp Worcestershire sauce • salt & pepper

Method: Mix all ingredients together in a bowl and form into 6 patties. Wrap in cling film and chill in fridge for 30 minutes. Fry on high heat (grill or pan) for 3-4 minutes on each side.

JD onion relish: • 4 large onions • 3 cloves of garlic, chopped • 2 tbs Evoo • 4 tbsp brown sugar • 2 tbsp Italian herbs • 1 can chopped tomatoes • ½ cup (120ml) BBQ sauce • salt to taste • 2 shots Jack Daniels

Method: Heat oil in skillet, add onions and fry until translucent. Add brown sugar and stir until it dissolves. Add garlic, mixed herbs and tomatoes. Simmer for 4 minutes. Add BBQ sauce and Jack Daniels. Simmer for another 10 minutes and season with salt.

Assembly: Fry your burger on the grill and place a piece of your favorite cheese on the patty 40 seconds before you remove it off the grill. The Jack Daniels onion relish should be placed on the bottom half of the bun, then place your patty on top of that, next, your tomato, topped with a healthy portion of rocket followed with the top half of the bun – "Ahhh-The Good Life!!!"

Curry Up Now

Husband and wife Akash and Rana Kapoor started Curry Up Now (with no formal training) in 2009, with a mission to serve the street foods from their childhood to Bay Area residents. The pair have since become champions of the Area's food truck scene, with five Curry Up Now trucks. As if that wasn't enough success, they opened the first of their three restaurants in 2011. Of grumbling brick-and-mortar restaurateurs resenting the food truck revolution, Akash says, "These mom and pop places need to step up their game! Whether you're a food truck or a sandwich shop, people have to love your food, and you have to offer something that you can't get everywhere else!" Curry Up Now's sell-out dishes include the Deconstructed Samosa, 'Thee Unburger' and Mexican-Indian fusion treat, Aloo-Parantha Quesadillix. Despite influences from all corners of the globe, they make sure their flavors are still rooted firmly in India. "Even if you can't pronounce them right, we hope you like the dishes as much as we do." San Francisco clearly does!

CHICKEN KATHI ROLL
serves: 6

- 2 lb (900g) boneless, skinless chicken breast or thigh, cubed
- 2 medium onions, sliced thinly • ⅓ cup (80 ml) oil • 1 tsp red chili flakes
- 1 tbsp crushed ginger • 1 tbsp crushed garlic • 1½ tsp cumin powder
- 2 tsp coriander powder • ½ tsp garam masala • 3 green chilies, roughly chopped
- 4 medium roma tomatoes, diced • coriander leaves, roughly chopped
- 2 limes • salt to taste • wax paper

Wrap: • 6 medium flour tortillas • 4 eggs • black pepper & salt • red chili flakes

Method: Heat a heavy bottom shallow pan for 3-4 minutes on medium. Add oil, ginger and garlic paste, stir constantly for 1 minute, add the dry spices. Stir mix for 2-3 minutes. Add diced tomatoes, stir and cover till the tomatoes soften a little. Add the chicken, cover the pot and cook for 5 minutes, stirring occasionally. Remove cover and add green chilies. Cook chicken for further 5-7 minutes, stirring constantly. Once oil separates and water evaporates from the chicken, add coriander leaves.

Wrap: Beat eggs and add dry spices in a shallow mixing bowl.
Heat large well oiled omelet pan, pour in egg mix to cover the size of the tortilla.
Immediately put tortilla on the egg; cook one side at a time turning only once.
Remove tortilla and add 3 tablespoons of chicken mix.
Garnish with coriander leaves and a generous squeeze of lime juice.
Roll the kathi like a burrito in the wax paper.

FRANKIE'S COFFEE

The concept for Frankie's Coffee was a result of Londoner Emma Jenkins' passions for travel, coffee and most things vintage. Frankie is the name of her truck. "Frankie is cute. Through him I was able to establish my own business doing something I love – baking, working with coffee and connecting with people." Emma had always yearned to move to Sweden; she speaks the language, and she finds the sweeping landscapes irresistible. So one day Emma and Frankie took to the road. She had no idea what to expect. "Crossing the North Sea on a 37-hour voyage and driving across Sweden from Gothenburg in a vintage '70s Citroen van isn't something one does every day. In a vintage van it's good to slowly take in the surroundings!" The business has been a great success, as a result of Frankie – "he makes people smile and wave" – and her killer cooking skills. Her customers' enjoyment has made the whole risk worth it. "My home-baked cakes, slices and cookies commonly cause a symphony of 'Mmmm' and 'Wow, this is so good'...followed by a smile from cake filled cheeks!"

FRANKIE'S CARROT CAKE
serves: 8-10

- 10 oz (300g) self-raising flour • ¼ tsp baking powder • ¼ tsp bicarbonate of soda
- 1 tsp ground cinnamon • 1 tsp nutmeg • pinch of salt • 4 eggs (whisk 2 together, separate 2 into yolk and whites) • 1½ cups (350ml) sunflower oil
- 7 oz (200g) brown sugar • 7 oz (200g) white sugar • 5 oz (140g) carrots, grated
- 4 oz (120g) walnuts, chopped • 1 tbsp boiling water

Icing: • 5 oz (150g) softened butter • 7 oz (200g) cream cheese
- 10 oz (300g) icing sugar

Method: Butter and line a large loaf tin and dust with flour. You will need a small, medium and large bowl. Preheat oven to 350°F (180°C). In the medium bowl sift together flour, baking powder, bicarbonate of soda, spices and salt. Whisk 2 of the eggs in the small bowl. In the large bowl beat together oil and sugar. Add the 2 beaten eggs slowly while beating and add the remaining two egg yolks. Stir in grated carrots and the chopped walnuts. Fold in the flour mix from the medium bowl a bit at a time, making sure it's thoroughly mixed through. Add boiling water a little at a time until the mixture stirs easily. In a clean small bowl, whisk the 2 egg whites to soft peak stage and, finally, fold them into the batter. Put batter in the lined tin.
Bake for 45 minutes. Allow to cool.

Icing: Mix all ingredients together until smooth, halve the cake and spread in one third of the icing mixture in the middle layer. Use remaining for the top. Sift a little nutmeg or cinnamon on top before serving.

THE CINNAMON SNAIL

Few food trucks are more famous than NYC's The Cinnamon Snail. Named one of *New York Post*'s Top Trends (and a Vendy Cup winner), there is something about this vegan, organic, Kosher truck that has captured the hearts of food truck lovers everywhere. Eccentric chef and founder Adam Sobel believes that the quality of his "certified orgasmic catering" initially reels people in. "Most of my customers come to my truck and see awesome looking donuts and pastries. They are not (yet) vegan and they fall in love with the sweet, donut-y circles of heaven. And I get to lure people into the non-violent lifestyle whether they want that change in their life or not!" Adam gives his dishes weird names like The Ultra-Right Wing Conservative Bearded Lady Bop. Despite The Cinnamon Snail's huge success, it is perhaps the extreme playfulness with which Adam and his team run their business that earns it its place in the nation's heart. "How are we going to go through the rest of our lives if we're not having fun with it? We have to have fun!"

KOREAN BBQ TOFU TACOS
serves: 4-6

Gochujang roasted tofu filling: • 2 tbsp gochujang (Korean chili paste) • 3 tbsp sesame oil • 2 tbsp maple syrup • 1 lb (450 g) firm tofu.

Method: Preheat oven to 400°F (205°C). Line a pan with parchment paper and lightly oil its surface. In a mixing bowl, whisk together the gochujang, sesame oil and maple syrup. Cut the tofu into strips, (¼ inch thick, ¾ inch wide, 2 inches long (0.5 x 2 x 6 cms). Toss the tofu in the marinade, to cover all sides. Arrange the tofu strips onto the baking sheet, leaving a little space between each. Bake for 15-18 minutes until golden-brown and a little crispy.

Sriracha cream: • 1 scallion, minced • ½ cup (120ml) vegan mayonnaise • 2 tbsp sriracha sauce • 2 tbsp maple syrup

Method: Combine all in a bowl and whisk for 30 seconds.

Assembly: • 8 corn tortillas, 6 inch (15cm) size • 2 cups baby arugula • ⅔ cup kimchi, shop bought (without fish) • ¼ cup additional gochujang, • 3 tbsp toasted sesame seeds • ¼ cup scallions, thinly sliced
Using tongs, warm the tortillas by placing over a gas burner for about 10 seconds on each side. Stack and then lay out the warmed tortillas. On each spread about 1 tablespoons of sriracha cream, a small pile of arugula, 2-3 tablespoons of kimchi, and 4 strips of tofu. Optionally garnish each taco with additional gochujang, sesame seeds and scallions.

THE FAT SHALLOT

Sam Barron and Sarah Weitz are in love with food and eating. The two kindled a romance many years after leaving high school, discussing a shared commitment to all things delicious. Sam's career began in Chicago with a long tour of duty at the hugely celebrated Everest Restaurant, followed by time in Spain at the three-Michelin-star Martin Berasategui. Sarah and Sam then travelled throughout Europe and Asia working on small local farms, honing their culinary skills and eating the best street food. New Orleans beckoned as the next stop, where they cooked professionally and fell in love with the city's food and culture. The husband-and-wife duo are now back home in the Windy City putting their accumulated expertise to work. The Fat Shallot food truck brings delicious American classics to Chicago's streets, like the BLT, Buffalo Chicken, pulled pork or meatball sub, all served from their stunning vibrant, crimson truck.

PULLED PORK SANDWICH (COCHON DE LAIT)
serves: 6-8

• 2 bone in pork butts • 2 cups (475 ml) Louisiana hot sauce • 30 cloves garlic
• 8 jalapeños • 1 bottle porter or other dark beer • 2 tbsp kosher salt

Method: Score butts with a knife and rub evenly on all sides with salt. Place in a deep roasting pan, fat side up. Evenly distribute remaining ingredients around pork. Cover with foil and cook at 390°F (200°C) for 7 hours. Let rest 2 hours or until cool enough to handle. Pull into large chunks and smash roasted jalapeños and garlic cloves in with pork. Pour liquid over pork and keep hot until ready to serve.

Remoulade sauce: • 1 cup (240 ml) homemade mayonnaise (see page 115)
• 1 cup (240 ml) coarse grain mustard • 5 cloves garlic, minced
• 3 tbsp Louisiana hot sauce • 1 tbsp kosher salt

Method: Whisk all ingredients together in a bowl
Fat slaw: see page 119.

Assembly: The Fat Shallot uses a custom made demi-baguette, but any good crusty bread or baguette cut into lengths about 6 inches (15 cm) would be perfect.
Toast lightly till warm, but not too hard or crunchy. Slice the bread lengthwise and generously smear the inside with the remoulade sauce.
Take a large portion of the pork, 5-6 ounces (approx 150g), and place inside.
Top with about a ½ cup of the slaw, enough for every bite and 3 or 4 jalapeño rings.
Dig in and enjoy!

kogi

At Thanksgiving in 2008, Kogi BBQ was first rolled out as the little Korean-taco-truck-that-could, peddling innovative $2.00 Korean barbeque tacos on the streets of L.A.. Little did these truckers know that within a few short months, Kogi BBQ would become an icon of L.A. and US street food, a roving symbol of rebellion, independence and the belief that excellent food can be had on a dime budget. Their short rib taco – two crisply griddled, homemade corn tortillas, double-caramelized Korean barbeque, salsa roja, cilantro-onion-lime relish and a Napa Romaine slaw tossed in a chili-soy vinaigrette – so iconic to Kogi, would soon become an L.A. classic. Chef Roy Choi - who has since become a celebrity in his own right, making countless TV appearances and being awarded *Food and Wine Magazine's* Best New Chef - originally blended the Korean, Mexican and barbeque flavours that he knew best. "I was tapping into my own veins, digging deep into the base flavors that raised me on the streets of L.A.." Chased away by club owners and cops initially, the support for Kogi grew and a small army of fans helped them to go from one truck to five. Mention Kogi's name to any food trucker now and you will see the reverence this little truck has earned. It is the original gourmet food truck and has paved the way for daring, explosive street food ideas around the world.

KIMCHI QUESADILLA
serves: 6

• 6 flour tortillas, 12 inch (30 cm) • 2 cups kimchi, chopped • 8 each sesame leaf or shiso leaf • 4 tbsp sesame seeds, toasted • 8 tbsp butter • 4 tbsp canola oil • 4 cups shredded cheddar cheese

Method: Cook kimchi with butter and continue to stir over medium heat till caramelized and charred. Set aside. Oil pan or griddle and place tortilla on pan and add 1 cup of cheese on one half. Over the cheese layer ½ cup of kimchi, two ripped sesame leaves and sprinkle 1 tablespoon of sesame seeds over. Fold over empty half of tortilla to create a half moon. Continue to cook and flip over. The quesadilla should look blistered like a Neapolitan pizza. Cut and enjoy the drippy goodness....

"This dish started as a fun food for us to enjoy in the truck and it just hit the streets with a force. Its spirit comes from Koreatown."

EL TACO TRUCK

In Stockholm, there is one truck to thank above all others for bringing the worldwide food truck revolution to Swedish shores. The raging popularity of El Taco Truck - the first Mexican food truck in Sweden - has helped to relax strict laws in the capital that had cut the country off from the global food movement. Tattoo shop owner and Harley Davidson-builder Nikola and his buddy Bolle used their previous history in the restaurant business and, inspired by their journey to the US in 2011, they decided they wanted to bring street food and Mexican food back home. They searched for a while to find a Step van - the sort that tacos are often served from in the States - and by chance, they came across one on the streets of Stockholm. With a lot of reconstruction, and some pinstriping from Nikola, the truck was ready to start serving in 2012. "Because no one was selling food from a moving vehicle, people were amazed when we drove down the street," says Nikola. "Screaming and shouting, like it's a UFO." Now, just two years later, Stockholm is experiencing its own food truck craze. Nikola puts his desire to have a truck down to looking for a connection with the past. "I guess I'm reaching back to older times, when things were made with more quality and more slowly." El Taco's food has been recognised at an international level, with the recipe below making it to the finals of a recent British Street Food Awards.

SOL BATTERED SOFT SHELL CRAB
Tarantella Borracho
serves: 4

• 8 medium soft shell crabs • 1 cup flour • 1 egg, beaten • garlic powder • black pepper • 7 fl oz (200ml) light Mexican beer • Panko breadcrumbs • frying oil • newsprint
Accessories: • 8 corn tortillas, 6 inch (15cm) size • citrus mayo slaw (see page 119) • cilantro pesto (see page 115) • pickled jalapeños • deep fried mint • limes

Method: Mix the flour, egg, garlic, pepper and beer in a bowl. Adjust the consistency with the beer according to how you like your batter. Heat the frying oil. Be sure to use an oil that can withstand high temperatures. Pinch loose mint buds and drop into the frying oil for about 10 seconds. Carefully lift and place on paper to dry. Pour batter into a soup bowl and breadcrumbs in another. Take a crab at a time and dip it into the batter, then the breadcrumbs and slowly lay in the frying oil. Depending on the size of crab you have, let it fry for 2-5 minutes. Place on paper to cool. We recommend the small or medium crabs - they are a little easier to handle and get crispier. Serve on an open burrito with your favorite combination of any or ALL of the above!

FRITEZ

Owner Ruben Kruit ran an internet company for 20 years. By 2010 he was totally fed up and sold the business. He needed a drastic change of career and lifestyle – "preferably not in an office environment!" With his new-gained freedom and encouraged by the increasing craze for all things food truck, Ruben came up with his idea for a gourmet chip shop. He bought an old chip truck and equipped it with a huge, retro, lit-up sign, and turning it into the first 'Fritèz Haute Friture' food truck. In December 2012 he and his team had their first booking at the Swan Market in Rotterdam. Since then it has been a rapid ride of markets, festivals and food events. They now own two food trucks and Ruben has even opened a chip shop at a fixed location in Rotterdam. It is amongst the food trucks, however, that Ruben says there is the greatest amount of camaraderie and encouragement, with a real urge to strive for improving quality. "My mission it to change 'Fast Food' into 'Fast Good' with a concept that has soul and charm. My vision is that consumers are demanding more and more authenticity, sincerity and quality and that's what I want to achieve."

FRIET ZOERVLEISJ (Fries with homemade stew)
serves: 6-8

Fries: • 2 lb 2 oz (1kg) organic Agria potatoes

Method: Cut washed potatoes (no need to peel) into fries with a minimum profile of ½ inch x ½ inch (1x1 cm). Fry them in vegetable oil with a temperature of 300°F (150°C) for 4-6 mins until you hear them 'sing'. Do not fry to brown. Remove from the oil and shake dry. Cool back to room temperature. Refry for a few minutes, until crispy and gold in oil, at 360°F (180°C). Take out, shake dry again and sprinkle with sea salt.

Zoervleisj: • 2 tbsp dairy butter • 2 tbsp olive oil • 2 lb 2 oz (1 kg) organic stew beef • 4 onions • 2 cloves garlic • sea salt • 8 ground cloves • juniper berries • pepper berries • fresh thyme • laurel leaves • 2 carrots • 1 leek • 1 stick celery • 4 tomatoes • 7 fl oz (200 ml) red wine/ white vinegar • 1 tbsp apple molasses • 4 slices gingerbread

Method: Into a big casserole add butter and olive oil. Add chopped onions and crushed garlic. Cut the beef into pieces and add with salt and pepper. Fry at a high heat; once meat is browned lower the gas. Add chopped vegetables, spices, herbs, tomatoes, red wine and vinegar. This ensures enough moisture to cook the meat slowly. Put a lid on the casserole and leave meat to cook for 2-3 hours on low heat. When the beef is softened (and has recognizable thread structure) add apple molasses and gingerbread. This makes the stew less liquid and more syrupy – perfect when added to fries!

gastroPod

GastroPod was the first mobile gourmet dining concept in Miami. Chef Jeremiah, Miami-native and owner of the legendary Bullfrog Eatz in Wynwood, customized a vintage 1962 Airstream with the latest in modern culinary technology. The result is a roving gourmet kitchen unlike any in South Florida. Jeremiah built his reputation through exciting contradictions. His cooking is a rich combination of the common and the exotic; he draws heavily on Caribbean and Latin American traditions. GastroPod's constantly evolving menu combines the freshest seasonal fish, meats and produce with experimental preparation techniques, and it's always served up with a laid-back, homestyle vibe. Before taking the plunge with his own food truck, Jeremiah had an illustrious restaurant career. He worked at El Bulli in Spain (at the time the world's best restaurant), later at New York's WD-50, Spice Market, Café Grey and Aquavit, and also at Moto in Chicago; quite an illustrious list!

AREPA, STUPID SLAW, GOAT CHEESE AND GPOD SAUCE
makes: 20 arepas

Arepa: • 2½ cups (700g) masarepa cornmeal • 1 tsp salt • 2½ cups (600 ml) hot water • 2 tbsp melted butter • vegetable oil

Method: Stir salt into arepa flour. Pour hot water over flour and mix well with a wooden spoon. Stir in melted butter. Cover dough with plastic wrap and let rest 15 minutes. Make thin Colombian-style arepas: divide the dough into 20 pieces, and form into balls. Place balls between 2 pieces of plastic wrap and flatten with hands until 6 inches (15 cm) in diameter and ¼ inch (approx 0.5cm) thick, using your fingers to smooth out any cracks along edges. Place arepas on a cookie sheet, covered with plastic wrap. Heat a cast iron skillet on medium heat. Place ½ tablespoon butter in skillet. Cook arepas about 5 minutes each side. The surface should dry and form a crust. They will brown slightly, but do not let them brown too much. The thinner arepas are done when they have formed a nice crust, but are still soft on the inside.

gPod sauce: mayo (for fresh see page 115) + sriracha hot. Mix in as desired.

Assembly: Serve arepas hot off the griddle with stupid slaw (see page 119), crumbled goat cheese and gPod sauce.

Le Réfectoire

The burger was the first fast food classic to undergo a revolution in France. Two years ago, the first wave of Parisian food trucks started to hit the streets, and the gourmet burger – French-style – was the star. Valentine Davase recognized a huge shift coming to Paris, which had previously stayed firmly anti-food truck. Along with other famous Parisian trucks like Le Camion Qui Fume, Valentine started to attend every market, event and festival that would have her, selling her sumptuous, refined burgers out of a converted black truck. A typical Le Réfectoire burger uses the marbled Charolais beef which is emblematic of Burgundy and "100% French – like all our ingredients, of course!" Decadent toppings include beech-wood smoked bacon, emmental, sheep's cheese and goat's cheese roasted in honey. Valentine says "street food is a phenomenon that is popular worldwide and truly multicultural. This defines the philosophy of Le Réfectoire, which has taken its position as the Parisian response to this international movement." In 2013, Le Réfectoire crossed the Channel to represent France at the British Street Food Awards, where they won trophies for Best Burger and Best Dessert.

THE RÉFECTOIRE 'FIFI' BURGER
serves: 6

Ingredients: 1 brioche bun from your favorite baker • 5 oz (150g) minced meat, (Charolais or Limousin) 20 % fat • 1 red onion • 1 bunch of parsley • 2 white onions • 1½ oz (50g) Fourme d'Ambert AOP mild blue cheese • 1 lettuce • 1½ oz (50g) butter • 1 clove garlic • Sunflower oil • mustard • Tabasco • salt & pepper • 3 tbsp caster sugar • white vinegar • homemade mayonnaise (see page 115)

Method: Mix ground beef with the finely chopped parsley, a pinch of salt and a pinch of pepper. Create nice round and thick patties and reserve in the fridge. Slice the red onion, soak in white vinegar, add a spoonful of sugar, stir and refrigerate. Chop the white onion and sweat in a pan with a little oil and then add 2 tablespoons of sugar. Simmer until a nicely caramelized.
Make the mayonnaise (page 115), then add several drops of Tabasco, the finely chopped garlic and a tablespoon of sugar. Set to one side.
Butter the bun and put in the oven. Cook the patties in a hot pan for 1 minute 30 seconds. Turn over, cover the second side with Fourme d'Ambert, and cook for a further 2 minutes, placing a lid over the pan so that the cheese melts evenly.
Arrange the buns with a good spoonful of mayonnaise on each side, then 2 lettuce leaves, 2 tablespoons of caramelized onions, red onions then finally your patty with the melted Fourme d'Ambert and close !
Serve with lightly seasoned fries, parsley and parmesan cheese. Delicious!

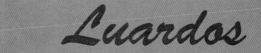

Luardos

Luardos has been a local lynchpin of food truck cooking for as long as Londoners can remember. It was the winter of 2006 when owner Simon Luard quit his temporary job at ice cream van Choc Star and opened up a refurbished Citroen H van as a burrito-bus. "I used to go to lots of festivals and was always disappointed with the Mexican food available," says Simon. Having spent time studying cooking in Oaxaca, Mexico, he realised he could offer explosively spicy and complex food, unknown in London at the time. It was love at first sight when he spotted a vintage 1969 Citroen H van - at the time a rare vehicle in England. On the first day of trading, the van nearly caught fire. Today Simon sells over 200 burritos a day, and has had rave reviews from from CNN to GQ Magazine. Luardos (named by making Simon's surname sound a bit Mexican) now has two trucks, also renowned for their incredible Day of the Dead exteriors.

LUARDOS' FISH TACOS
serves: 4

• 1 lb 5 oz (600g) Coley (filleted and sliced into 1 inch (2.5 cm) wide "fish finger" shapes) • 1 ³/₄ cups (500ml) groundnut oil • 1 ripe avocado, sliced • ½ ripe mango, finely diced • fresh cilantro (coriander), chopped • sliced fresh chilies/chipotles in adobo • your favorite hot sauce • 8 fresh corn tortillas, 6 inch (15 cm) • shredded cabbage

Pico de gallo salsa: see page 117 **Batter:** see page 123
Luardos "special" sauce: see page 114

Method: Make the batter, "special" sauce and pico de gallo salsa. Put to the side. Slice the avocado, the mango and chop the cilantro. Get a large saucepan, pour in the groundnut oil and heat to 350°F (190°C). Take the Coley fingers and dip them in the batter. Pull them out and let the batter drip off a little before frying them in the oil until they turn light golden-brown and crispy (about 3-4 minutes). Once cooked place them on kitchen towel and sprinkle with sea salt. Heat a frying pan.
Grab your corn tortillas and heat them in the pan with a tiny drop of the groundnut oil. Let them sizzle in the oil for about 15 seconds either side but don't let them go crispy.

Assembly: Place one piece of Coley on the tortilla, add some special sauce, some hot sauce and/ or fresh chilies according to your spice preference, some mango, a slice of avocado, a spoonful of pico salsa, chopped cilantro and shredded cabbage.
Fold it up in your hand and get stuck in!

SPECIALS
SIDES & EXTRAS

- Due to an illness in the family, V.S.F. IS CLOSING as a food cart! Our last day will be May 17th. THANKS for 4 AMAZING YEARS!
- PØLSE - Chicken sausage, Jarlsberg cheese, Dijon & Cole Slaw, wrapped in LEFSE - 7⁵⁰
- Rhubarb Wrap - Local rhubarb preserves, Portland Creamery Chèvre, walnuts & raw honey, wrapped in LEFSE - 5-

SIDES, ETC.
- Spiced braised greens
- Spring Potato Salad with peas & fresh herbs - 3-
- Sweet & Sour purple cabbage - 2-
- Pickled Herring in white wine - 3-
- Add BACON to ANYTHING - 1⁵²
- Side of MJØLLNIR - 50¢ (our own BEET based hot sauce, named after Thor's HAMMER!)
- Side of Local Lingonberries - 50¢

DRINK
- House-Made LINGONBERRY ICED TEA!
- 12 oz. - 2- • 20 oz. - 3-
- Plastic cup for WATER - 25¢

ORDER HERE!

FINAL WEEK HOURS:
WED 7pm - 8pm
THUR 12 - 8 pm
FRI 12 - 9 pm
SAT 12 - 9 pm

HOURS

PORTLAND OREGON

VIKING SOUL FOOD

When Jeremy first knew Megan, he noted that at Christmas her family had a tradition of making potato lefse. A lefse is a thin flatbread, rolled by hand and baked on a griddle; similar to a tortilla, it has a lighter texture and toasted potato flavor. Jeremy fell in love with this humble dish and saw its potential as a great street food. The pair realised they had a unique and versatile concept on their hands. In 2010 they purchased a 52-year-old Streamline Duchess aluminium silver trailer, naming her Gudrun, and opened Viking Soul Food on the streets of Portland, Oregon serving Scandinavian-inspired dishes in addition to lefses. Although the term 'soul food' is more commonly used to refer to food with African-American origins, for Megan and Jeremy, it means something more. "It is food that is almost indescribably comforting, makes the most of humble ingredients, and refuses to waste anything. That's what gave us the name of our company."

SURKÅL OR SWEET & SOUR CABBAGE

We serve this with our most popular dish, meatballs with Norwegian brown cheese.

makes: 3 lb (approx 1.4 kg)

- 1 densely packed or 2 not so densely packed heads purple cabbage
- ¾ cup (180 ml) apple cider vinegar • ¾ (180 ml) cup red wine vinegar
- ½ cup granulated sugar • ¼ cup ground caraway seeds, toasted
- ¼ cup fine sea salt

Method: Core and quarter cabbage. Slice it as thinly as you can, like you would for coleslaw. Lay it in a sturdy, heatproof plastic or glass container in 1 inch (2.5cm) layers. Sprinkle kosher salt over each layer. Allow to set for 1-2 hours as this will draw out moisture from the cabbage as well as soften it. Meanwhile, heat vinegars, sugar and ground caraway in a stainless steel or otherwise nonreactive pot (do not use aluminum). Bring to the boil and pour the mixture over the salted cabbage. Stir with a wooden or stainless steel spoon until thoroughly mixed. Allow to cool, then store in an airtight container in the fridge. Taste the cooled surkål to be sure the salt/sugar levels are to your liking. You should get a little kick from the vinegar at first, but that will mellow out over the course of a week or two.

Surkål, like most pickled vegetables, will keep for months.

WAFELS & DINGES

Tireless and affable describes Thomas DeGeest, the owner of NYC's Wafels and Dinges. Formerly an IBM consultant, he is today the self-styled Special Envoy for Wafels (this is the native spelling) for the Belgian Ministry of Culinary Affairs. Way ahead of the food truck revolution curve, Thomas and his wife used their entrepreneurial spirit to take the streets of New York City by storm in 2007. Employing all their culinary knowledge, business acumen and vibrant personalities - and spinning a story about being sent by Belgium to rescue the sorry state of America's waffles - they began to sell delicious, genuine, Belgian treats to rapturous New Yorkers. Thomas has since become something of a celebrity, appearing countless times in print and on screen - including on CBS and Food Network's *Throwdown! With Bobby Flay*. The truck has gained considerable critical acclaim, winning a coveted Vendy award for Best Dessert.

WMD A.K.A. WAFELS OF MASSIVE DELICIOUSNESS

The "classic" WMD is a light and crispy Brussels waffle topped with strawberries, chocolate fudge and whipped cream. Many customers have developed their own custom version of a WMD, and so over time WMD came to mean "any waffle with as many toppings as you'd like" – all for $7. Some people really go to town and make a point of loading up on every single topping ("dinges") on the menu. Belgians typically don't put a lot of toppings on their waffles. Traditionally, this may have been because the waffles were really a poor man's harvest celebration; another explanation may very well be that the waffles, as a pastry, can stand on their own (as opposed to American Belgian waffles, which are more like tasteless slabs of dough used to transport piles of toppings to their destination).

serves: 4-6

• ½ cup (120 ml) warm water • 1 tbsp active-dry yeast • ½ cup butter
• 2 cups (500 ml) milk • 2 tbsp sugar • 1 tsp salt • 3 cups all-purpose flour
• 2 eggs • baking soda

Method: Add yeast and water in a large mixing bowl, stir and let stand for a few minutes. In a separate bowl combine melted butter with the milk, salt and sugar. The liquid should be lukewarm before adding it to the dissolved yeast mixture. Add the flour and stir until the dough is smooth and gloopy. Cover with plastic wrap and let it sit on the counter overnight to double in volume. The next morning, beat the eggs together and add baking soda. Combine into the batter with a whisk. Heat waffle iron until steaming and grease if not non-stick. Cook the waffles until golden-brown.

Assembly: Slice fresh strawberries on top, whipped cream (we place two dots), drizzle chocolate and ALWAYS finish with powdered sugar.

MOZZA & CO

In 2012, Parisians Arthur Gambard and Thibault Merendon had a simple idea for a food truck: to celebrate that most irresistible of Italian cheeses – mozzarella. They kept their vehicle small, building a delightful serving station on the back of a reworked Vespa scooter. From this they started to sell tasty salads and focaccia, made using four different types of top-range Italian mozzarella, as well as traditional Italian desserts like tiramisu and panna cotta. "Sophistication and Italian savoir-vivre are the key words," says Arthur. Mozza & Co. is now known as one of the trendiest truck spots in Europe; recommended by the likes of *Condé Nast Traveller* and *Harper's Bazaar*, tourists and hipster locals flock to Arthur and Thibault's permanent spot by the Musée d'Orsay. "It is with the sweet charms of Italy that we draw people in," says Arthur. "That and the allure of our majestic enchantress, mozzarella!"

FOCACCIA WITH BUFFALO MOZZARELLA
serves: 4

The success of this recipe is largely down to the quality of the ingredients so there is no better place to start than a top-notch Italian deli.

• 2 focaccia • ¼ lb (100g) crushed fresh tomatoes • herbes de provence • extra virgin olive oil • Grana Padano, thinly shaved (Parmigiano Reggiano will do) • 6 oz (200g) mozzarella di bufala affumicata (lightly smoked) • 10 slices speck dell'Alto Adige (lightly smoked dry cured ham, leaner than prosciutto but the latter will do) • rocket

Method: Cut the bread in half horizontally. Crush tomatoes with a splash of olive oil and a pinch of herbes de provence. Add a thin layer of the crushed tomato to the bread base and sprinkle with petals of Grana Padano. Cut the mozzarella balls into ¼ inch (approx 0.5 cm) slices to create the next layer (be generous). Place on a couple layers of speck and cover with rocket. Add the top of the focaccia and toast. This can be done on a griddle turning every few minutes until the outside is crispy and the inside ingredients melt in the mouth. If you are feeling like going to town try drizzling with fresh homemade pesto.

MOTHER CLUCKER

After spending six months developing and taste-testing the perfect fried chicken in 2013, business partners Ross Curnow and Brittney Bean decided to bring their English-meets-American recipes to the London food truck scene. They first trialled their tea-brined chicken at a few parties in London's trendy Dalston and Shoreditch neighbourhoods. The Cluck Truck (an ex-US army ambulance) then made its first, highly anticipated public appearance, and is now permanently parked up and frying in Ely's Yard, next to Brick Lane – London's Mecca for hipster shoppers. Served up with hearty and delicious Southern American and Caribbean-influenced sides like Rice N Peas and Cajun fries, along with a healthy portion of chicken-related puns (the truck's Twitter handle is @cluck_you), this is fried chicken at its informal best. Try their crunchy chicken strips with black-eyed peas if you want to see why *Time Out London* named this truck home to one of London's most indulgent dishes. Clucking divine! (Sorry – hard to stop).

AL'S MAC AND CHEESE
serves: 4-6

• one bag of Macaroni pasta shells • 2 cloves garlic, finely chopped • 1 white onion, chopped • 3 courgettes, cut into half moon shapes • 4 oz (125g) salted butter • 1 cup plain flour • splash of white wine • 2½ pints (1.2 l) milk • 1 lb (500g) mature cheddar • 3 oz (100g) pickled jalapeños, chopped (more if you like it spicy) • Panko breadcrumbs (2 handfuls) • salt & pepper

Method: Turn oven on to gas mark 6 or 7/ 320°F (160°C).
Boil the pasta and set aside. Lightly fry off onion on medium heat for a couple of minutes, add garlic, jalapeños and courgette and cook a further few minutes then set aside (you don't want the courgette to soften too much). Melt the butter into a pan and stir in the flour to form a paste. Let out with a little white wine then add milk slowly, stirring for 10-15 minutes until sauce thickens. Add cheese on a low heat and mix. Season to taste.
Add the macaroni to the mix and stir in gently. Add cooked garlic, courgettes, jalapeños and onions. Grab a baking tin and lightly oil. Slide the mix and pasta into the tin and spread evenly. Sprinkle extra cheese and bread crumbs on top, cover with tin foil. Bake for 15 minutes then remove tinfoil and bake for a further 15 minutes until nice and crispy on top.

BOOM!

MAXImus miniMUS

The idea for Maximus/Minimus came to self-trained chef Kurt Beecher Dammeier when, one day, he brought in pulled pork sandwiches for the office staff at wholefoods company, Sugar Mountain. Whilst experimenting with menu concepts, he came up with the idea of a food truck offering sandwiches with yin-and-yang flavor profiles. Inspired by his nickname for his son Max, he decided Maximus was to stand for the spicy elements in his dishes and Minimus for the sweet. After having settled on a concept and a name, Kurt says, "it was a wild ride turning the truck into an 'urban assault pig.'" He worked with a local Washington designer to ensure the pig truck met his vision of being cool and unexpected without being ridiculous. Since Maximus/Minimus opened for business it has earned some seriously high praise – including being nominated as one of America's 15 best food trucks by relish.com.

BRAISED PORK
serves: 6-8

- 3 lb (1.4 kg) pork shoulder, trimmed and cut into 1½ inch (4 cm) cubes
- 2 tbsp paprika • 1 tbsp kosher salt • ½ tbsp freshly cracked black pepper
- 3 tbsp extra-virgin olive oil • 3 tbsp rice vinegar • 10 large garlic cloves, roughly chopped (about ⅔ bulb) • 2 large yellow onions, roughly chopped

Method: In a large bowl, stir together the pork, paprika, salt, and black pepper until the pork is coated in the spices. Heat 2 tablespoons oil in a large pot over medium-high heat. Add just enough pork to nearly cover the bottom in one even layer. Let cook for 30 seconds or until browned. Turn the meat and continue to cook until it has browned evenly, about 7 minutes, stirring occasionally. Be careful not to burn the meat.

When the meat has fully cooked, remove it to a separate bowl and add 1 tablespoons olive oil to the pot. Continue cooking the remaining meat in the same fashion until it is completely cooked through. Depending on the size of your pot, you will cook two to three batches. When you have added the last of the meat, there may be some remaining spices in the large bowl. Reserve these spices for use later.

When the last of the meat has cooked through, add 4 cups (1 litre) of water to the pot and stir to deglaze. Put the meat that has been set aside back into the pot. Add the reserved spices, vinegar, garlic and onions. Stir until the ingredients have all mixed in.

Increase the heat to high and bring to a boil. Reduce to medium heat and let cook for 50 minutes. Reduce heat to medium-low, cover and continue cooking for 20 minutes. The meat is done when it pulls apart easily with a fork.

If you come from Orange County, CA, you may know the ornately decorated truck from which Hop Phan and his team serve up their delicious, Latin-Asian fusion food. Hop credits his Vietnamese grandmother for his lifelong passion for food and L.A.'s Komodo truck for inspiration. It took a terrifying accident though to convince him that there was no time to waste. "I was driving to my second job one night when I was hit. It really shook me up and was my wake-up call that I needed to do something with my life." After buying a truck and having it emblazoned with designs from local tattoo artists, Bad Influence Tattoo Inc., Hop worked on his menu. With dishes like Vietnamese Chimichurri and Korean Mexican BBQ Beef, it isn't hard to see why Dos Chinos has been so popular. And the name of the truck? "'Chino' is how many Spanish speakers refer to anyone Asian. If you grew up here you would get it and not be offended" says Hop.

OAHU SHRIMP
HAWAIIAN GARLIC BUTTER SHRIMP
serves: 2

- 16 shrimp • 2 soft tortillas, 10 inch (25 cm) • 2 tbsp ghee • 8 cloves garlic, minced
• dash fish sauce • sea salt & fresh cracked black pepper to taste
Garnish: • fresh diced pineapple • shaved red cabbage • onion, slices
• cilantro, chopped • cilantro crema (see page 113)

Method: Never get pre-peeled shrimp. For a really nice Latin-Asian shrimp taco, burrito, wedges, quesadilla or shrimp fries use large to medium large size shrimp, headless with shell-on. Most shrimp that are available to the general public are frozen and preserved with certain salts. The shells actually protect the flesh of the shrimp from the full effects of the preserving salts and when you peel, butterfly, and de-vein your own shrimp you will notice a huge difference in quality, even with frozen shrimp. Clarified butter or ghee creates an intense buttery flavor – perfect to sauté the shrimp. In a large saucepan on medium heat add the ghee. Once bubbling pour in the shrimp and stir gently for 4-5 minutes making sure that the shrimp are evenly cooked. Add garlic, fish sauce, salt and pepper and sauté for 1 or 2 additional minutes, maximum.

Assemby: Heat the tortilla on one side on a hot griddle. Flip over and while on the heat add the shrimp and diced pineapple. Before it gets too crisp transfer to a plate and sprinkle with onion, cilantro and a generous zig-zag of crema.

El Porteño

Joseph Ahearne grew up in Napa, California, as part of a family deeply connected to the area's buzzing food and restaurant scene. His mother, originally from Argentina, taught Ahearne the family recipe for empanadas. His sister, who had a stint as a pastry chef, helped perfect the empanada dough for El Porteño. The result is a fluffy, flaky crust that is similar to French pastry dough rather than the harder, drier crusts that one often finds with empanadas. Joseph also uses local and seasonal ingredients, including Prather Ranch organic dry-aged grass-fed beef, Fulton Valley all-natural chicken, organic Far West Fungi mushrooms, local chard and homemade Dulce de Leche. Since starting the business back in 2009, Argentine expats and local devotees alike have lined up at markets and on the streets to get their hands on these tasty handheld pies. Now El Porteño also has its own kiosk, located in downtown San Francisco's historic Ferry Building.

While Ahearne has big aspirations for El Porteño, he says, "like most Argentines I'm not in any hurry."

EMPANADA DE CHAMPIÑONES
makes: 20 empanadas

- 6 cups grated parmesan cheese • 8 tbsp butter • 8 tbsp olive oil
- 4 cup shallots, thinly sliced • 3 lb (1.4 kg) mixed Far West Fungi wild mushrooms, roughly chopped • salt & pepper to taste • 1 cup (250 ml) dry white wine
- 2 cups (500 ml) vegetable broth • 2 cups (500 ml) crème fraîche
- 1 cage-free egg, for wash • 20 empanadas (see page 123).

Method: Preheat oven to 350°F (175°C).

Filling: Wash and chop mushrooms. Slice shallots thinly. Roughly chop butter. Heat butter and oil in a large skillet over medium heat. Add shallots and cook until golden, about 5 minutes. Stir in mushrooms, salt and pepper and cook until soft, 6 to 8 minutes. Add wine and broth and simmer. Stir often, until liquid has almost evaporated, 6 to 8 minutes more. Stir in crème fraîche and simmer until liquid has evaporated further, about 10 minutes. Remove from heat and cool in ice bath, stir frequently to cool faster. When cold, fold in parmesan.

Empanadas: Spoon 2 oz (60g) of filling onto half of each empanada; press lightly to flatten, leaving ½ inch (1.25 cm) border. Brush with egg wash around filling on one tapita half. Lightly sprinkle coarse sea salt (about 8-10 grains) evenly. Fold plain pastry half over filling, stretching dough to cover. Seal edges with fork tines. Repeat to form remaining empanadas. Transfer empanadas to parchment paper-lined sheet pan, spacing 2 inches (5 cm) apart. Press edges of empanadas again with fork tines. Brush empanadas with egg wash. Bake for 10-15 minutes or until golden-brown.

STREET KITCHEN

London chefs Mark Jankel and Jun Tanaka started Street Kitchen in 2011 in a single Airstream trailer, serving bistro-style takeaway lunches to busy Londoners; they now have a fleet of three across the capital. They have added epicurean breakfasts to their menu and are even exploring a new Asian street food concept, which would use 100% UK meat and vegetables. Fresh produce is extremely important to Mark and Jun, and they scout out the best suppliers for the food they want to serve, like Capel Mushrooms or "the lovely Daphne from Elwy Valley," who supplies them with naturally-reared and supreme quality lamb, which Mark and Jun slow cook for 12 hours and serve with English pesto and pickled seasonal vegetables. Despite huge critical and commercial success, Street Kitchen is always on the lookout for a new challenge. They say, "Nothing excites us more than being given a brief that challenges our creativity." When it comes to catering from their vintage Airstream, Street Kitchen is renowned for its bespoke menus and service style.

GRILLED MACKEREL WITH BEETROOT AND HORSERADISH DRESSING
serves: 4

- 4 mackerel fillets, boned • 12 oz (350g) potatoes • 2 oz (50g) butter • 4 beetroots
- 1 tbsp white wine vinegar • 1 tbsp sugar • handful of mustard leaves
- horseradish dressing (see page 115)

Method: Wrap the beetroot in aluminum foil and bake in the oven at 355°F (180 °C) for 2 hours. Remove from the foil, place in a bowl, cover with cling film and leave for 30 minutes, then remove the skin with your hands. Cut into bite-size segments and place in a clean bowl with the vinegar and sugar. Season to taste. Cook the potatoes in boiling salted water until soft. Drain, place in a bowl, add the butter and lightly crush with a fork. To cook the mackerel, pour a little rapeseed oil in a non-stick pan, season the mackerel and carefully place, skin side down into the pan. Cook for 3 minutes then flip over and cook for a further 2 minutes until firm.

Assembly: Spoon some potato into a box, add the beetroot beside it, top with some mustard leaves and a fillet of mackerel.
Finally finish with a drizzle of horseradish dressing.

MS P'S ELECTRIC COCK

Take one outrageous name, a larger-than-life silver Airstream trailer, some high-wattage branding and a very flamboyant chef-owner and you've pretty much got Ms P's Electric Cock. Now an institution in Austin, Texas, Ms P ("a.k.a. P Momma") started up the business partly because she couldn't understand the lack of places nearby selling great fried chicken. She had grown up in the tiny west-Texas town of Tahoka and acquired her love of food and cooking from her mother and great grandmother –"Big Mama" – who taught her how to cook Southern-inspired "stick-to-your-ribs" food. Cooking remained Ms P's primary passion, even as she went on to pursue a successful career in sales. Then, she says, in 2010, "after my husband Kyle and I suffered a devastating tragedy, I re-evaluated my aspirations and left sales to follow my true love – cooking for others." Her idea was to capture the nostalgia of a simpler time experienced during her childhood in Tahoka, "when food was field-to-fork, and friends and family gathered in the kitchen to share smiles and conversation while simply enjoying flavorful food."

MS P'S DIRTY BLACK EYED PEAS
serves: 6

• ½ lb (230g) raw pepper bacon, diced • 2 cups onions, chopped • 2 smoked ham hocks (scored on each side to release smokey flavor), 3-4 oz (approx 100g) each
• 2-3 tbsp garlic, chopped • 4 bay leaves • 5 sprigs of fresh thyme
• 1 lb (450g) dried black eyed peas • 10 cups (2.4 l) chicken stock • salt & pepper

Method: In a large pan, over medium to medium high heat, render the bacon until crispy, about 4 to 6 minutes. Add the onions and sauté for 2 to 3 minutes until brown and translucent. Season the onions with salt and pepper. Stir in ham hocks. Sauté for 2 minutes. Stir in the garlic, stirring for 2-3 minutes. Add bay leaves and thyme, or a sachet for easy removal. Add black eyed peas and chicken stock to cover peas and allow enough liquid to evaporate. Bring the liquid to a boil and reduce to a simmer or as I call it "a giggle not to be confused with a laugh". Cook for about 1 ½ to 2 hours or until the peas are just tender. Do not over cook it as the peas will break and turn mushy. Remove peas from the heat and ham hock from the peas and pull away tough skin, fat and pork meat. Separate the pork meat, shred and then add back to peas.
Ladle into bowls and serve with sour cream, crispy bacon and chives.
Delicious with sweet corn bread or crusty bread.

CHINGÓN

"On virtually any street corner in Mexico you can find people gathering amongst the aromas of fresh tortillas, wood smoke, roasted vegetables, toasted chili and grilled meats," say brothers Mick and Will Balleau. After moving permanently to Melbourne in 2010, they decided to open a restaurant called Chingón as a celebration of the flavours, decor and music they grew up with in New Mexico. Chingón is, according, to the brothers, "a Mexican slang word that encompasses all things agreeable, good, beautiful, notable, likeable, respectable, or just plain badass." After the runaway success of the restaurant it only made sense to build a mobile version, and in 2012 they opened their Taco Truck. This is not just any truck – it is an old Jayco caravan in awe-inspring, hand-beaten copper, with a menu and logo adorned with Hot Rod flames and stripes. From this they now offer soft tacos, charred corn, salsas, spicy soups and sopa seca to passers-by on the streets of Melbourne.

TACO AL PASTOR
(CHARGRILLED PORK AND PINEAPPLE TACO)
serves: 6

- 2 lb 2 oz (1 kg) pork tenderloin • warm corn bread • chipotle crema (see page 113)
- queso fresco (available from latin grocers or substitute with a crumbly feta)
- 6-10 wholemeal soft tacos

Pork marinade: 1/8 cup (30ml) chipotle en adobo • 6 cloves garlic • 4 tbsp (60g) achiote paste • 3½ tbsp (50 ml) apple cider vinegar • 2 tbsp honey • 1 bunch fresh cilantro (coriander), chopped • 2 tbsp olive oil • 2 tsp salt • 2 tsp ground black pepper •

Method: Place the pork in a large bowl. Add the marinade ingredients and toss to coat. Cover with plastic wrap and place in the fridge overnight. Before cooking make the pineapple salsa (see page 117). Cut the pork into thin strips, about the thickness of a minute steak. Heat a barbecue or chargrill to a medium-high heat. Cook the meat for 1 minute per side.

Corn Base: 8-10 ears of sweet yellow corn, shucked (canned corn can be used but for best results shuck your own!) • 2½ oz (75g) of butter • 1 tsp salt

Method: Char-grill corn until slightly blackened. Remove kernels, boil for 15 mins. Stir in melted butter and salt. Set the corn mixture to one side and keep warm.

Assembly: Once the pork is cooked, shred with a fork. In warmed soft tacos add the warm corn base and chipotle crema, pineapple salsa and queso fresco. Sprinkle a pinch of chipotle powder over the top

FRESH ROOTZ

It's pretty hard to miss Andrew Phazey's and Martin Brooks' much admired, upcycled, converted caravan ("The Shack", constructed by friend Digby Platt) from which they serve their extraordinary vegetarian food in Leamington Spa, UK. There is much more to this truck than its rustic beauty, though: the prestigious British Street Food Awards recently crowned their crisp pakoras Best Snack. Martin and Andrew say their ethos is to "use British root vegetables and turn them into contemporary world fusion dishes." They are inspired both by their travels all over the world (with unique tribal village recipes influencing their flatbreads) and their work with people with learning disabilities. Collectively they have over two decades' experience of working in Mental Health, and say caring for adults and young children has showed them the vital importance of a good diet and healthy eating.

CARROT, SESAME SEED AND ORANGE CEVICHE SALAD
serves: 6 side dishes

- 10 medium carrots • 7 tbsp mixed black and white sesame seeds, toasted
- 2 oranges, juice of 2, zest of 1 • 1 tsp cilantro (coriander) seeds • 1 tsp cumin seeds
- ½ tsp chili flakes • 1 tsp Mesquite meal • 1 tbsp dark brown sugar
- 1 bunch of cilantro, roughly chopped • good pinch of salt & pepper

Method: Grate carrots then toast the cilantro and cumin seeds in a dry pan on a medium heat for 1 to 2 minutes, careful not to burn. Once toasted put into a pestle and mortar and grind to a fine power. Combine all the ingredients together in a bowl and leave in the fridge for an hour, then serve.

Die dollen Knollen

Die Dollen Knollen is fast becoming one of Berlin's most recognizable foodie attractions. Recommended by publications from *Traveller* to *Vogue*, this French Citroën HY Van has charm, class and *kartoffelpuffer* to die for. For those that haven't tried it, the truck specializes in crispy, low-fat potato latkes (potato pancakes). They are simple and delicious (with the 'Reinheitsgebot' consisting of potatoes, egg, gluten-free flour, salt and a little nutmeg) and come with a variety of original toppings - like quark with grated carrots, beetroot crème or smoked fish. Alexander Boder and Angelika Thielemann arrived in Berlin from Austria in 2001 and a long-term crazy idea between friends became a great plan, which they put into action in 2009. Since then, the truck has gone from strength to strength, but they have always remained faithful to their shared environmentalist principles: all of their packaging is compostable and their potatoes are 100% locally sourced, reducing the amount of fuel and travel time.

POTATO LATKES
"Crispy, gracefully designed, low fat and gourgeous-tasting"
serves: 6-8

- 2lb 2oz (1 kg) baking potatoes, peeled, thinly grated • 1oz (25g) gluten-free flour
- 1 free-range egg, beaten • salt & freshly ground black pepper
- freshly ground nutmeg • olive or vegetable oil, for frying

Method: Place the grated potato into a colander and squeeze out as much moisture as you can. Mix the potatoes with the flour, egg and salt and freshly ground black pepper, and a hint of freshly ground nutmeg. Heat the oil in a frying pan until moderately hot and then place heaped tablespoons of the mixture into the pan to shallow fry. Lower the heat to medium, flatten each latke with the back of a spoon and fry for about 4 minutes on each side, turning over when the edges turn golden-brown. If the heat is too high, the latkes will become dark-brown on the outside before they are cooked in the middle. Remove the latkes from the pan and rest on brown paper bags (not only will the paper absorbs the oil - it leaves the latkes crisper).

Assembly: Serve the latkes hot with anything from soured cream and herbs, to smoked salmon and lime-cream.

HEISSER HOBEL

Originally located in Allgäu in southern Germany's Swabia, Heisser Hobel is now at the vanguard of Berlin's burgeoning food truck scene. Named after the grater used to create the cheesy, doughy delight that is Spätzle, Heisser Hobel serves these rich, traditional, German treats by the truckload. Co-founders Florian Rohrmoser and girlfriend Myriam Tucas initially wanted to sell something that represented their native Allgäu region, so set to work on developing the ultimate Spätzle recipe. "We freshly prepare everything," says Florian, "from the dough to the finished dish. I use a big pot with boiling water into which I grate the dough of the Spätzle. We mix it all with three different kinds of cheese." Their cheese comes from Florian's parents' cheese factory, where everything is still handmade. Florian says if he had to choose a film title to describe their life inside the truck, it would be German war epic *Das Boot*: "because we fight some battles in here - all this cooking in a very limited space - and at the end of the day we are totally exhausted but the truck is still intact!"

KÄSSPÄTZLE
serves: 6-8

Dough: • 2 lb 2oz (1 kg) flour • 6 eggs • ⅔ cup (350 ml) water
• 1 tsp salt (depending on salt in water)
Method: Mix the ingredients together to make a dough. Kneed the dough with your hands until smooth and elastic. Cover and let it rest for 30 minutes.

Onions rings: • 2 large onions • 1 oz (30g) flour • pinch paprika powder • 3 oz (85g) butter
Method: Cut onions into rings. Add flour and paprika to a bowl and coat the onions evenly. Put butter into a pan on medium and fry the onions until golden.

Kässpätzle: • boiling water • 1 tbsp salt • 10 oz (280g) cheese, grated
(we use Mountain cheese and Emmental, but Gruyere is also good)
• 1 oz (30g) butter • fresh chives

Method: Heat a large pan of salted water. You will need a Spätzlehobel (large grater) or a colander with big holes that you can fill with dough and grate into the boiling water. Keep the water boiling gently on medium low. The spätzle will come up to the surface within seconds. Let them boil another 30 seconds then lift them from the water with a slotted spoon. Repeat until completed. Empty water and heat butter and return the hot Spätzle to the pan and stir in with the cheese until the cheese has completely melted.

Assembly: Put the Kässpätzle on a plate with some of the onions on top and garnish them with fresh chives and black pepper. That's it.

Korilla BBQ

Korilla was founded by Edward "3D" Song, pioneer of the NYC food truck explosion, Queens kid, and Columbia grad. When Korilla was a mere concept, Eddie partnered with the Weitzel twins of SoHo's digital agency, Box Creative, to help with the marketing. It wasn't long before Korilla was rolling out their third truck, had won Rookie of the Year at the Vendy Awards, received incredible press, reviews, and fans, and eventually broke ground at their first brick and mortar location. "Our little tiger cub grew up fast!" says Eddie. "We've braved the mean streets (and mean cops) of NYC, sold tacos and burritos worldwide, rocked classic kids' show *Sesame Street*, and were on reality TV's *The Great Food Truck Race* on The Food Network." Their menus have grown up too. Today they offer the best quality proteins, kimchi, and vegetables they source locally, as well as seasonal specialities and the occasional secret menu. They say all-natural, healthy, GMO-free, and fresh aren't just marketing terms, they are their responsibility. "We've redefined what you know about Korean Barbeque. Korilla brings you the best of Korean cooking, in a format you already love. In other words, a burrito with bulgogi and bacon kimchi fried rice has been your favorite burrito all along!"

BACON KIMCHI FRIED RICE (BKFR)
serves: 4

• 4 cups one day old cooked rice • 8 slices thick cut smoked bacon, sliced into 1 inch (3 cm) pieces • 3 eggs lightly beaten • ¾ cup kimchi, roughly chopped • 2 tbsp kimchi liquid from your jar of kimchi • ½ onion, diced • cooking oil

Method: Heat cooking oil in a wok over high heat. Add the diced onions and stir until cooked. Remove the onions from the wok and put in a bowl on the side. Scramble the lightly beaten eggs until mostly set, but not over cooked. Remove the eggs from the wok and add them to the bowl with the onions. Cook the bacon until crisp. Remove and put in the bowl with the onions and eggs. Add the rice to the wok, stirring occasionally until all the clumps are broken down and the rice is heated through. Add the onions, eggs, bacon and fry until all ingredients are mixed throughout the rice. Add the chopped kimchi.

MeSoHungry

As the name suggests, Me So Hungry is a truck that offers meals of monster proportions. Since launching in September 2012, their XL burgers and delicious sliders have become so popular that they are now staples of music festivals like Coachella, as well as on the streets of L.A., Orange County and San Francisco. "We're experts in delivering the 'sneak attack'," say founding brothers Mike and Cory Ewing. "Bold flavors, fiery sauces, unlikely combinations, and new foodie specials for our dedicated followers." Gourmet standards and responsible sourcing are important to executive chef, Cory. "We change our menu seasonally. Like many of the world's finest restaurants, our regularly changing menus ensure that only the highest quality and freshest ingredients are used in our monster dishes." Chef Cory has been trained at the world-famous Le Cordon Bleu culinary school and has worked at such high-end establishments as The Four Seasons hotel. However, he says his is a laid-back, less-is-more approach, and this is why it suited him to start up a food truck, where he could focus on letting a few dishes shine and giving him the chance to interact with the public. "I take cues from my love for the outdoors and I specialize in grilling, seafood and international cuisine."

MESO BURGER
serves: 2

- 14oz (400g) aurora ground angus chuck (20% fat) • 4oz (115g) sharp cheddar cheese
- 4 strips apple wood smoked bacon • 4 slices tomato • 3oz (85g) mixed field greens
- 5 fl oz (150 ml) meso asian BBQ sauce • 2 brioche buns, 4 inch (10 cm) • salt & pepper

Method: First cook bacon till crispy. Cook burgers to desired wellness. Season with salt and pepper. Melt cheese on the patty, toast buns. Put BBQ sauce on top and bottom of buns, place tomatoes on both sides, then meat and cheese, place strips of bacon, lettuce and top it off with the bun. Serve with lightly dressed field greens.

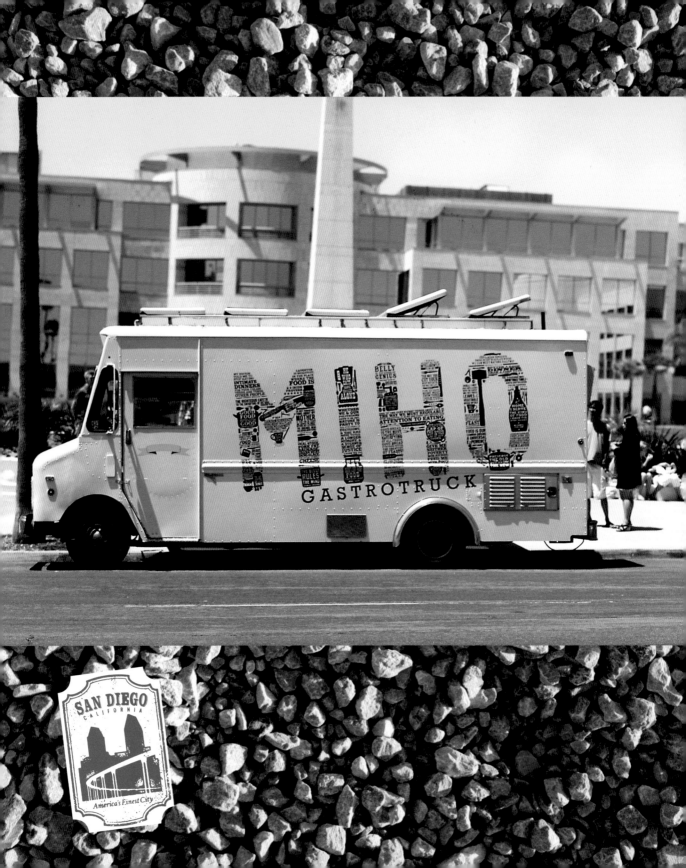

MIHO

Kevin Ho and Juan Míron started MIHO in 2010 because they wanted to bring a better quality bite to their neighborhood. "We don't buy anything processed. It's real food." The pair's farm-to-street food philosophy finds its roots in an honest, handmade approach to each and every meal. "We make everything from scratch with the same love and care that our family of local farms uses to grow the finest organic and naturally raised ingredients." Never afraid of a challenge, Kevin and Juan decided early on that they would change their menu daily, according to the freshness of their produce. Their seasonal menus feature an exciting selection of hors d'oeuvres, appetisers, entrées, salads, sides, desserts and refreshments. Great care has gone into each dish – of the kind one might expect to see in a Michelin-starred kitchen. MIHO was recently named Best Food Truck by *San Diego Magazine*.

FRIED CHICKEN AND BISCUIT RECIPE
serves: 6

Biscuits: • 4 cups all-purpose flour • 1 tsp salt • 1 tsp sugar • 1 tbsp +1 tsp baking powder • 1 tsp baking soda • ½ lb (225g) unsalted butter, cut into cubes and chilled • 1 ⅓ cup (315 ml) buttermilk

Method: Preheat oven to 425°F (215°C). Mix dry ingredients and butter in food processor and then add the buttermilk by hand. Don't over work the dough. Roll and cut in squares or circles with cutter. Bake for 20 minutes and brush with melted butter as soon as they come out of the oven.

Chicken: 2 lbs (900g) boneless and skinless chicken thighs • 3 cups (700 ml) buttermilk • 1 cup seasoned flour (cinnamon, cayenne pepper, black pepper and cumin)

Method: Brine the chicken (see below) for 24 hours. After that time discard the brine and place the chicken in the buttermilk for one hour. Get a fryer up to 350°F (175 °C). Coat each piece of chicken with the seasoned flour and fry until it reaches 165°F (75°C).

Brine: 3 cups (700 ml) water • 4 tbsp kosher salt • 4 tbsp brown sugar • 4 cloves • 1 pinch cinnamon • 1 star anise • 1 tsp mustard seeds • 1 tsp cumin seeds • 1 tsp chili flakes • 1 bay leaf • 2 cloves garlic, smashed

Method: Boil all the ingredients. Once cool it's ready to use and lasts up to two weeks.

RAINBO

Xochi Balfour first met fiancé Ben Sheinwald a year after she graduated. She says they immediately bonded over a shared loathing of tedious work colleagues, limited holiday and pointless Excel spreadsheets - "among far lovelier things." Making the decision to pack in their much-detested 9-to-5 lives, in March 2011 they got the job of running British street food advocate Petra Barran's chocolate van over the summer. Enamoured with the buzz of street serving and the itinerant lifestyle, in September the pair turned their thoughts to serving their own creations. Both love healthy but satisfying food, and their beloved gyoza (Japanese dumplings) seemed to do the trick perfectly. They came up against many walls starting out. "Money was in limited supply and everywhere we went we were faced with the widespread (and ridiculous) belief that if you jump off the career ladder you will never, ever, get back on, and will be left to fester in a pit of regret and misery having wasted a good education." Now the proud owners of a unique, converted truck, critical acclaim, a coveted spot at London's KERB and one of the most ethical food trucks around (with 20p from every sale going to fight child labour in Nepal), we think it's pretty safe to say these ex-white collar workers have never looked back!

CHICKEN AND CILANTRO GYOZA
makes: 40 dumplings

- 10 oz (300g) Napa cabbage, chopped • 10 oz (300g) chicken thighs, minced
- 2 oz (70g) cilantro (coriander), chopped • 1 tbsp finely grated ginger
- 1 tbsp sesame oil • 1 tbsp sake • 1 pack 40 gyoza skins • 2 tbsp vegetable oil
- 1 tbsp soy sauce • 1 tsp rice wine vinegar • 1 tsp salt

Method: Sprinkle the cabbage with the salt, mix with your hands and set aside for 10 minutes. Combine the chicken, cilantro, ginger, sesame oil, sake and some salt and pepper in a bowl. Rinse the salt water off the cabbage, then squeeze out as much of the liquid as you can. Add the mince to the cabbage. Cover and chill for 30 minutes. Spoon 1 teaspoon of the mixture onto a gyoza skin. Dip your finger into a bowl of water, then wet the rim of the skin. Fold the skin in half and join the edges. Place the dumpling on a plate. Continue until all of the filling has been used. Heat the oil in a large frying pan with a lid. Place 20 or so dumplings in the pan. When the gyoza begin to brown on both sides, add ½ cup (100ml) water and cover with the lid. Steam for 4 minutes, adding more water if necessary. Remove the lid and allow the dumplings to sizzle for 1-2 minutes or until the gyoza turn light brown and crisp. Repeat for the next 20 dumplings. Serve with a dipping sauce of the soy sauce mixed with the rice wine vinegar.

SCHMEAR IT

Schmear It is Philadelphia's - and possibly America's - first philanthropic bagel truck, donating a portion of its sales to a new local cause every two weeks. What leads one to become a "Chief Schmearer?" Apparently in founder Dave Fine's case, there aren't necessarily any of the tell-tale signs. Hailing from Baltimore, Maryland, Dave is a proud fan of the Orioles, Ravens and *The Wire*. He attended the University of Pennsylvania where he studied History, Communication, and a bit of Psychology on the side. "Whilst at Penn, I got to know and love Philly, especially its rich food scene." He also tried his hand at the non-profit sector, working for Community Health Charities of Maryland. He says this combination of experiences led to a particular interest in leveraging business and branding for social good. Schmear It is Dave's first project in social entrepreneurship. The Bagel Mobile began life as "an empty shell, it's really just a recycled delivery truck." To build and retrofit it as a food truck, Dave turned to Philadelphia's Executive Auto Salon. Here, Dave worked with them to design the Bagel Mobile, determining everything from the shape and placement of the window to layout of kitchen equipment and electrical output. Aside from good looks and great causes, Schmear It prides itself on seriously good bagel sandwiches - from tried-and-true seasonal specials to build-your-own Dream Schmears.

STUFFED FRENCH TOAST SCHMEAR
serves: 6-8

- 2 cups (475 ml) cream cheese • 1/3 cup banana, diced • 1/3 cup strawberries, diced
- 3 tbsp maple syrup • 3 tbsp walnuts, chopped • 1 tsp ground cinnamon

Method: Toast walnuts in a dry pan on medium-low heat until they are just golden and the aroma fills the air. Use a rubber spatula to gently mix strawberries, bananas, maple syrup, cinnamon, and walnuts in a medium bowl. Once the ingredients are well mixed, add cream cheese and stir with more force until the ingredients are well incorporated.

Assembly: Schmear on fresh bagels, french toast or waffles and enjoy.

VOODOO VAN

After years of rocking crowds in music venues (and much to the surprise of both friends and fans), in 2011 the members of San Francisco-based 'dirty sex rock' band Flexx Bronco started a food truck called Voodoo Van. Although band-member-turned-food-truck-impresario Phil Stefani says he doesn't have a history in cooking, he certainly knows what he likes when it comes to street food. "Being in a touring rock band, as well as a bartender, I love street food or late night food on the go. I always wanted to open a bar or venue but I love travelling and I can't stand that feeling of standing still." The early days of the food truck revolution signalled the perfect option for Phil. The ethos of the band's truck has been important for all members. The proudly printed motto on the van is "No forks, No knives, No mercy," and Phil says this is what street food is all about. "You eat it with your hands. You're gonna get messy." The team call their brand of food "Cosmic American", inspired by the style of music popularized by the legendary Gram Parsons, and the food that they have tasted whilst touring across the States. Both Phil and bandmate Kevin have Cosmic American tattoos. They are serious about providing an eclectic mix of American food for their punters, to show the rich mass of influences from which the US has benefited. Their menu might at any one time include Skirt Steak, a Seitan Sando, JuJu Balls and oh-so-naughty but delightful desserts.

THE KONG
FRIED PEANUT BUTTER SANDWICH
serves: 4

Sandwich: • 8 slices white bread • 2 bananas • crunchy peanut butter • marshmallow fluff • salt • powdered sugar • coco krispies cereal

Method: On one half of the bread spread peanut butter, on the other spread the marshmallow fluff. Slice banana half into 9 pieces and place evenly on the fluff side. Lightly salt the banana fluff side, put the sandwich together. Repeat.

Crêpe batter: • 5 oz (150g) flour • 6 fl oz (175 ml) milk • 5 fl oz (150 ml) water • 1 large egg, cage-free • canola oil for frying

Method: Heat canola oil in a deep pot or fat-fryer. Whisk flour, milk, water and egg together till mix is thick but not goopy. Should be thick enough to coat and stick to sandwich. Drop sandwich in batter and be sure to cover the edges. Take sandwich out and roll in coco krispies. Gently place sandwich in frying oil. Flip floating sandwich over so it gets an even fry. Take sandwich out and let is sit on brown paper to cool down and allow excess grease to soak away. Slice in half or quarters. Cover in powdered sugar.

TACOFINO

In 2012, after two highly successful years in Tofino (a cool, ex-hippy port on west Vancouver Island), acclaimed taco vendors Tacofino decided to take their truck and head for the bright lights of Vancouver. It was not as simple as arriving and setting up shop though. The City Council there is so stringent about allowing only the best possible food trucks to operate that a panel of judges carefully screens every potential truck – using members of the council, the culinary world, the media and the public to make their assessment. Luckily, Tacofino bowled over the panel with their Baja-inspired tacos, and won their license to take to Vancouver's streets. They have since been described in the media as selling "the best Mexican, or at least the best fish tacos in British Columbia." Tacofino's wonder-chef Kaeli Robinsong says, "Tacofino was born out of a desire to create a unique dining experience and take the Baja-style taco to another level." Their offerings include 'Tuna Ta-takos,' Roasted Squash Tacos and Wild Mushroom Quesadillas. The truck itself wows locals, with its vibrant, bright orange exterior, which Vancouver artists Lee Robinsong and Robert Mearns have cleverly adorned with a painting of the Virgin de Guadalupe holding a taco.

CHOCOLATE DIABLO COOKIES
{Recipe by Kaeli Robinsong and Amy Bockner}
makes: 12 big cookies

- 1½ cups all-purpose flour • 1 cup cocoa • 1 tsp baking soda • 1 tsp cinnamon
- ½ tsp cayenne pepper • 1 tsp salt • ½ cup (120 ml) canola oil • 1 cup white sugar
- 1 cup golden sugar • 2 eggs • 1 tbsp vanilla extract
- 3 tbsp freshly squeezed ginger juice

Method: Sift together flour, cocoa, baking soda, cinnamon, cayenne pepper and salt. Whisk separately oil, sugar, eggs, vanilla and ginger juice. Add to dry ingredients and mix. Scoop 2 oz (60g) dough balls onto a greased cookie sheet or parchment paper, spaced out well as they spread! Push your favorite chocolate chunks or chips into them and sprinkle with white sugar and rock salt. Bake at 375°F (190°C) for approximately 15 minutes or until they crack.

LA POPOTE

Perrine Goutx and Deborah Stöhr are an inseparable duo. Now in their thirties, they first met ten years ago, when they both dreamed of making it in the culinary world. Several years of working front of house at various restaurants confirmed their love of gourmet cuisine and genial hospitality. Those years also gave their private project time to ripen and, encouraged by the worldwide mobile food revolution, in 2013 they decided to open their own food truck. "We wanted to embark on an adventure," says Perrine, "and spend our time at the controls of our own travelling canteen." Deborah is of Swiss heritage, and has always been immersed in the world of gastronomy - her mother being a styliste culinaire and her father a restaurateur (today based in Bali). The duo decided to pair the influences of Deborah's family with the French tastes of Perrine's and apply traditional Franco-Swiss flavors to US favorites hot dogs and pretzels. Their unique signature dish is veal sausage and grilled pork with coleslaw, caramelized onions, cheddar, pickles, ketchup and mustard, served in a pretzel-shaped brioche "wheel," made exclusively for them by their master baker, Master Julien. Deborah and Perrine decided to launch their truck in the Gulf of Saint Tropez, which despite its renown, lacked in their view a great offering of fresh and healthy cuisine. Waitressing is long-forgotten, and they would never swap the "freedom to create, to please customers, to be nomadic and to meet people."

HOTDOG "LE POPOTE" (OUR MOST POPULAR!)
makes: 1 hot dog

• 1 hot dog bun (we use a bun made by our artisan baker; if you're using off-the-shelf, get the best you can) • 1 white bratwurst sausage (Swiss style) • ⅔ oz (20g) of English Cheddar • 1 onion • 1 portion of coleslaw (see page 119) • ½ tsp brown sugar • slug of balsamic vinegar • pinch of curry powder • pinch ginger • pinch tumeric • 1 medium/large gherkin • mustard • ketchup • salt and pepper

Method: First prepare the mayonnaise (see page 115). Grate the cheddar and finely chop the onion. Heat some olive oil in a pan. Add the onion, salt, pepper, tumeric, brown sugar and balsamic vinegar. Reduce until the onion is well caramalized. In a separate pan grill the sausage for a few minutes on a high heat. Turn down and heat for 10 minutes longer, or until the skin turns golden and crispy. Finely slice the gherkin and add a little honey, curry powder, ginger and salt and pepper. Mix well.

Assembly: Slice open the bun. Add ketchup, mustard, coleslaw, cheddar and pickled gherkin, followed by the grilled sausage. Finish by adding the caramalized onions. Eat immediately!

Suggested accompaniment: home fries cooked in beef fat.

Naked Frog

After working as an architect and designer for many years, Christian Gaubert, proud owner of Marseille's Naked Frog, can now finally say, "I am living for my passion." His passion was inspired by his French mother Niçoise, his Swedish wife and his attraction to Asian food - a style of cuisine he says has traditionally been nomadic. After working at a few highly regarded Marseille restaurants, Christian took the plunge. He chose a beautiful 1972 Citroën HY, "this legendary post-war vehicle, which equipped the artisans, firefighters, police officers and the Tour de France." He named her Jojo. Christian then narrowed down his choice of regular menu to varieties of that delectable Argentine classic, the empanada, although at certain events he also serves anything from Provençal stew and veal ragu to marinated salmon and black pudding macaroons. Christian says, "our favourite frog hits the road to take you on culinary journeys of multi-cultural, refined gastronomy."

EMPANADAS DE CARNE SUAVE
makes: 20 empanadas

Dough: 1 lb 2oz (600g) flour • 2 oz (50g) butter, melted • 6 tbsp olive oil • 1½ cups (350 ml) water • 1 tsp salt

Method: Sift flour, dig a well and add the remaining ingredients. Add water until you obtain a compact ball. Let stand at least 1 hour in the refrigerator.
Flour the work surface. Roll out the dough. Cut discs 8 inches in diameter.

Filling: • 1 lb 1 oz (500g) ground beef • 1 lb 1 oz (500g) white onions, cut into small cubes • 1 red pepper, cut into small cubes • 1 green pepper, cut into small cubes • 1 bunch spring onions (green and white), sliced • 1 tbsp paprika • 1 tbsp dried oregano • 1 tbsp cumin • 1 tbsp cinnamon • 1 tbsp aji molido (Argentine hot red pepper) • 2 egg yolks • salt & pepper • olive oil

Method: Start cooking the onions in olive oil, add the peppers and cook on low heat for 10 minutes. Add salt, pepper and spices. Turn up the heat and add the meat. Cook on low heat for 10 minutes, cool. Add the spring onions, mix well.

Combine: Preheat oven to 480°F (250°C). Place a soup spoon of stuffing in the middle of each empanada. Fold together the two sides and seal with a fork. Put the empanadas on a tray in the oven and reduce the temperature to 390°F (200°C). Cook 8-9 minutes. Remove from oven and wash with egg yolk. Return to oven to bake for a further 6-7 minutes. They are ready when golden.

BANH MI BOYS

The brainchild of management-consultant-turned-Masterchef-contestant Keen Poon, lawyer Francis Fung and Chinese medicine doctor Darren Kwok, Banh Mi Boys is the Vietnamese truck that is taking Melbourne's buzzing street food community by storm. 'Banh mi' means bread in Vietnamese, although the bread most commonly used there is a baguette-type loaf, which the Banh Mi Boys use for their sumptuous sandwiches. Originally inspired by their travels to Southeast Asia and the tastes, smells and colors of Vietnam, their food – cooked fresh from the truck – takes a spin on the traditional, whilst using modern Asian flavors and techniques. The Boys guarantee, "it will rock your taste buds," and hordes of Melbourne fans seem to agree. Try their fresh and herby Best Mate Salad or their Lemongrass Pork Belly Banh Mi – a toasty baguette loaded with chargrilled pork belly, pickled carrot, cucumber, coriander, gutsy aioli and spicy dressing.

VIETNAMESE ORANGE AND GINGER CEVICHE
serves: 6 starters

Marinade: • 4 oranges, juiced • 1 lime, juiced • 1 small knob ginger, finely grated (about 1 tbsp)
Method: Combine the citrus juices together in a large cup and add ginger to marinate for 30 minutes before use.

Desiccated coconut: • 3½ oz (100g) desiccated coconut • 2 tbsp fish sauce • 1 tsp sambal olek chili
Method: Preheat oven to 300°F (150°C). Stir fish sauce and sambal chili through coconut and ensure even distribution. Place coconut mixture on a flat oventray lined with baking paper and bake in oven for 20 minutes.

Ceviche fish: 12 oz (400g) blue cod / cod / snapper (we use Chatham Island Blue cod) • 1 semi-ripe mango, finely diced • 5 kaffir lime leaves • 2 tbsp salt • 12 betel leaves

Method: Lightly rub salt on fish and leave on for 5 minutes before washing off. Thinly slice fish into sashimi-style slices and place carefully into a deep plate. About 20 minutes before serving pour marinade over the fish to ensure just enough to cover fish. After 20 minutes remove fish and evenly distribute onto a neat pile of betel leaves. Add a little bit of marinade to provide moisture and a few slivers of ginger.

Assembly: For garnish thinly julienne kaffir lime leaves and finely dice mango. Right before serving place a small portion of mango on top of fish, some coconut and a sprinkling of kaffir lime leave julienne on top.

Wholefood Heaven

Wholefood Heaven is run by husband and wife team David and Charlotte Bailey. David is a classically-trained chef who has worked in some leading London restaurants including Vong, E&O and Eight over Eight. In 2005, Dave made the decision to become a vegetarian – a radical choice for a chef. He has never looked back, both in terms of health and personal fulfilment, and has since worked as a consultant to nearly all of the top vegetarian restaurants in London, in addition to acting as personal chef to a number of high-profile clients. Wife Charlotte is an Oxford graduate who has spent many years working in the natural health industry. She is a qualified homeopath and is a lifelong vegetarian. In 2009, they started their own produce business, Wholefood Heaven, from their house in Camden, London. They quickly became increasingly involved in London's vibrant, burgeoning street food scene, taking their healthy and high-quality food to the masses via a converted Citroën H van. They have since scooped the award for Best Main Dish at the British Street Food Awards and have recently been featured in the BBC's *River Cottage Veg* with Hugh Fearnley-Whittingstall.

GLASS NOODLE SALAD

This vegan glass noodle salad is one of our absolute favorites for a light lunch or dinner and is absolutely packed to the rafters with all the colors, flavors and vibrancy of South East Asia.
Vegan, wheat and gluten free.
serves: 1

- 4½ oz (125g) glass noodles (rice vermicelli), dried • 1 carrot, cut into thin strips
- 3½ oz (100g) mange tout, cut into thin strips • 1 oz (30g) cilantro (coriander), fresh
- 4 limes, juice of • 2 cloves garlic, finely chopped • 1½ oz (40g) ginger, finely chopped
- 1 red chili, deseeded and finely chopped • 3 tbsp brown sugar • ½ tbsp tamari
- 5 oz (150g) mixed sprouts (eg mungbean, chickpea, lentil) • sesame seeds, lightly toasted • 3½ oz (100g) smoked tofu, thinly sliced

Method: In a bowl, pour boiling water over the glass noodles and leave to soak for 4 minutes. Strain and then, under the tap, allow cold water to pour over the noodles until they have cooled down. Make sure they're fully strained and then leave to one side. To make the dressing, in a pestle and mortar, crush together the garlic, ginger, chili and sugar until they resemble a paste. Add the lime juice and tamari and stir. In a large bowl add the carrot, mange tout, coriander, sprouts, smoked tofu and noodles. Gently mix together by hand before pouring over the dressing and then continue to mix by hand until the dressing has been well incorporated. Sprinkle over the toasted seeds and serve.

the Bowler

The Bowler delivers great balls: meatballs, fishballs and vegballs. This original London street food truck now brings ballsy flavors and handmade wares to streets, festivals, film sets, parties and weddings all over the UK. Succulent spheres of free-range pork, chicken and British beef are ground from whole cuts, dropped in fresh sauces, served with wild rice, pastas, polenta or in subs and sliders. Jez Felwick, chef and owner, first got on the path to owning his grassy, green van when he took a sabbatical from work and went to cookery school on an organic farm in Ireland. Seeing the food truck revolution in the US convinced him to pack in his job for good, put his balls on the line and try his hand at gourmet street food. The Bowler has since repeatedly been named one of London's top food trucks by national newspapers, magazines and global TV channels like CNN.

BEEF & CHORIZO BALLS
serves: 6-8

• 2 tbsp olive oil • 1 small garlic clove, crushed • 1 large egg, cage-free
• 1lb 1 oz (480g) beef chuck steak, minced • 7 oz (200g) cooking chorizo, sweet or spicy,
finely diced • 14 oz (400g) white rice, cooked weight, 3½ oz (100g) uncooked; you can
omit this and add more breadcrumbs • 7 oz (200g) Manchego cheese (or cheddar),
coarsely grated • 1 tsp smoked paprika • 3½ oz (100g) breadcrumbs
• 1 lemon, grated zest • 1 tsp salt • 3 tbsp chopped parsley

Method: Preheat the oven to 425°F (220°C), gas mark 7 and line a baking tray with non-stick baking parchment. Beat the egg in a large bowl. Add the minced beef, garlic, chorizo, rice, cheese, smoked paprika, breadcrumbs, lemon zest, salt and parsley and mix with your hands until well combined.
Heat a small frying pan over a high heat. Break off a small amount of the mixture, flatten between your fingers and fry until cooked. Taste to check the seasoning and add more if necessary. Form the mixture into balls each about 2 inches (5cm) in diameter, packing each one firmly, and place them on the prepared baking trays. Bake for 15–18 minutes, turning the trays halfway through – the balls should begin to brown on top. Keep an eye on them to make sure that they don't get burnt underneath where the cheese melts.

Assembly: I often serve these Bap 'n' Ball style. Get a bread roll of your choosing (I like a toasted ciabatta or brioche burger bun). Then spread on some tomato sauce, and mayo. Add the meat, some green leaves (rocket, etc), sliced gherkins or pickles and some cheese, which you can melt under a grill or grate on top.
Devour, but be sure to have some napkins to hand.

HIX'S FISH DOG

Celebrated chef, restaurateur and food writer Mark Hix is renowned for his original take on British gastronomy. After 17 years as Chef Director at Caprice Holdings (a group which encompasses the illustrious Ivy) he opened his own - Hix Oyster & Chop House in London's Smithfield - to great acclaim in 2008. He has since opened a further six (soon to be seven) establishments including 'Tramshed' in London's hipster Shoreditch (complete with its very own cow-in-formaldehyde-vat centrepiece by his friend, Damien Hirst) and of course, HIX Soho. Mark turned to street food as the food truck revolution swept through the nation's capital, choosing a delightfully humble - and British - classic: the breaded fish finger sandwich. When Mark is not dishing up food across the capital, he is penning a monthly column in *Esquire Magazine*, a weekly column in *The Independent* newspaper, and his best-selling cookbooks on British cuisine.

FISH DOG

- 1 lb (450g) thick white fish fillet like cod, coley, pollack • flour for dusting, seasoned
- 1 egg, beaten • 1½ oz (45g) fresh white breadcrumbs • vegetable or corn oil for frying
- 4 large soft torpedo rolls or hot dog buns, halved

For the mushy peas: • 1 oz (30g) butter • ½ lb (230g) frozen peas, defrosted
- 3½ fl oz (100ml) vegetable stock • a few sprigs of mint, stalks removed
- salt and pepper

For the Tartare sauce: • 2-3 tbs homemade or good quality mayonnaise (see page 115)
- 10-12 small gherkins, roughly chopped • 1tbs capers, rinsed and chopped
- a squeeze of lemon juice

Method: First make the mushy peas: put the peas, vegetable stock and mint leaves in a saucepan, season and simmer for 4-5 minutes. Blend in a food processor or liquidiser until smooth with the butter. Check and correct the seasoning. Keep warm. Mix all of the ingredients together for the Tartare sauce.

Cut the fish into long fingers the size of the roll. Have three bowls ready, one with the seasoned flour, one with the eggs and the third with the breadcrumbs. Lightly coat the fish in the flour, shaking off any excess, then pass through the egg and finally the breadcrumbs.

Heat the oil in a frying pan and cook the fish for a 2-3 minutes on each side until crisp and golden then remove and drain on some kitchen paper. Spoon the mushy peas on the hot dog bun, lay the fish on top with some tartare sauce (or serve separately).

Place the top of the bun on and serve immediately.

CARB & NATION

Fata Wijaya and Kevin Micheli were sous chefs at Church & State in downtown L.A. (one of Jonathan Gold's top 101 restaurants) until they opened Carb & Nation's doors in April 2014. On starting the truck, they say, "what started out as a conversation on how to put together the perfect burger quickly turned into a study of various types of bread, sauces, cooking techniques, flavour combinations, and textures that would work together to enhance the experience of eating a sandwich." They used their Le Cordon Bleu training and experience working in three-Michelin-starred kitchens to find the best possible flavour sandwich and soda flavour combinations – both traditional and new. They take pride in their flatbread that comes from freshly-made dough, which they press and bake to order on their grill. "It has been a challenge to speed up the execution of our made-to-order gourmet sandwiches at fast-food speed, but trust us: it is definitely worth the wait!"

MISO GLAZED PORK BELLY

- 2 lb (900g) pork belly

Miso Glaze: • 10 fl oz (300 g) Soy sauce • 1 lb 5 oz (600 g) honey • 4 tbsp ginger • 3 tbsp garlic • 5 oz (140 g) miso • 1 tsp Thai chili
Method: Put all ingredients in a blender and blend until smooth.

Brining liquid: 3½ oz (100 g) salt • 3½ oz (100 g) brown sugar • 1 tbsp black peppercorn • 1 tbsp maple syrup • ½ tsp coriander seeds • ½ tsp cloves • 2 star anise • 1 gal (3.75 l) water
Method: Mix everything in a pot and bring to a boil then let it cool. Submerge the pork belly in the brining liquid for at least 12 hours.

Cooking liquid: ½ cup (120 ml) soy sauce • 1 cup (240 ml) sake • 1 cup (240 ml) mirin • 6 scallions, sliced • 6 cloves garlic, smashed • tbsp ginger, sliced • 1 shallots (sliced).
Method: Bring everything to a boil.

Cooking pork belly: Put the brined pork belly in a metal container that can be safe to cook in the oven. Bring the cooking liquid to a boil before pouring it into the pork belly (make sure the pork belly is completely submerged). Wrap with foil, place in the oven for +/- 3 hours.

Cooling down: Once pork belly is completely cooked and tender, move it to a sheet pan, wrap it with a plastic wrap, and put another sheet pan on top. Add something heavy on top of the sheet pan to weigh down the pork. Once it's cool, you can slice it to your desired thickness.

Glazing the pork: Sear both sides of the sliced pork in a sauté pan until golden brown. Add a good slug of miso glaze mix. Allow it to reduce until the pork looks well glazed.

DUB PIES

Kiwi Gareth Hughes' journey, from Master's degree in Psychology to founding DUB Pies, has been a fascinating one. Not sold on any of the numerous jobs he tried after college - including, in addition to more corporate posts, some stints as a radio DJ and a New York cabbie - he enlisted to manage counsellors at an NYC disaster assistance centre following the devastation of 9/11. After a year of this, Gareth was emotionally and physically burnt out and returned to his native New Zealand for a break. It was whilst munching on his home country's unofficial national dish that he realised the answer to his career question - "and perhaps the answer to every question" - was pies! After first starting an extremely popular Brooklyn storefront café in 2005, he launched New York's first savoury pie truck in 2014, with the help of a generous Kickstarter fundraising campaign. The truck has a frequently changing offering of deliciously hot DUB Pies, both savory and sweet, including classics like Steak Mince & Cheese and Curry Vegetarian. Gareth partners with dedicated fair trade providers Counter Culture Coffee, to present some of the very best coffee available in NYC - "and certainly the best available on a food truck!" They're particularly proud of their flat whites. The team also have a range of NZ-inspired sweets including lamingtons and ANZAC cookies, plus cold drinks including Brooklyn Soda Works and Kombucha Brooklyn. It certainly looks like this is the truck New York has been waiting for. DUB Pies has already been labelled one of the best food trucks in NYC by *Business Insider*, *Time Out New York* and the Vendy Awards.

THE DUB PIE TRUCK BRUNCH PIE
makes: 1 x 5 inch (12.5 cm) oval pie

• Short crust pastry - as needed • crisply cooked bacon - two well cooked rashers, chopped • 1 whole XL egg • White Vermouth • Cheddar grated - as needed • puff pastry - as needed • egg wash - as needed

Method: Line a 5-inch (12.5 cm) oval pie tin with short crust pastry. Line bottom of pie with chopped bacon. Break egg over bacon, being careful not to break yoke. Top with a little grated cheese - don't over do this as it can cause the lid to pop off while baking. Moisten edges of short crust pastry with water. Place puff pastry on top, cut to fit and press to seal. Cut slits for steam to escape. Brush with egg wash. Bake at 350°F (175°C) degrees until pastry is golden and cheese is melted and egg cooked, about 30 minutes.

Suggested serving condiment - a generous dollop of HP Sauce!

THE CHILI PHILOSOPHER

"If America had a national dish, it would be chili. Chili is as American as a bald eagle. It's as American as the cattle trail that prompted its creation and the diverse immigrants that concocted it." When England-born Alex Kavallierou moved to the States, he was shocked to find that although chili is celebrated with annual cook-offs in every state and county, and every region has its much-loved variation, there was no chance of going to a local chili restaurant and eating his favourite dish. Chili restaurants just didn't exist. Alex put his mind to rectifying the situation, and started up the first gourmet L.A. food truck "taking the humble bowl of chili to the next level." Alex serves his triple beef chili with freshly baked cornbread using state-of-the-art methods and farm-to-truck suppliers. His chili burger is a chili-infused-patty and the flavors of his pork chili are inspired by the Asturias region of Spain. The truck's philosophy is simple: to perform every stage of cooking to its absolute fullest, so that Alex's team can make The Chili Philosopher the best of its kind in America. And L.A. locals are already queuing up in their droves outside this unusually decorated truck, which shouldn't be too hard to find. Just look for the face that Alex describes as a mixture of "Charles Darwin, a *True Grit*-style cowboy, and the most interesting man in the world."

TURKEY CHILI
serves: 8

• 3 tbsp tomato paste • 1 tbsp Thai red curry paste (you can make your own or buy a good brand like Mae Ploy) • 3 lbs (1.4 kg) ground turkey • 1 can pinto beans, drained. • 1 tbsp lime juice • 2 tbsp Thai palm sugar • 2 tsp fish sauce • water • 3 tbsp corn oil • 1 onion, finely diced • 1 bell pepper, cored, deseeded and cut into strips.

Method: Heat oil in saucepan. Add diced onion with a pinch of salt and sweat until translucent. Add curry paste and cook out for 5 minutes.
Add tomato paste and red bell pepper cut into strips and cook out for 5 minutes.
Brown turkey in a separate pan and add to the saucepan. Add water to cover and bring to a boil. Add palm sugar, lime juice and fish sauce.
Drain brine from pinto beans and add the beans to the saucepan.
Simmer for up to four hours. Taste for seasoning. Serve with cilantro (coriander), grilled sweetcorn and sour cream. We add coconut to our sour cream to complete the Thai-influenced flavors. And, of course, serve cornbread on the side! (see page 123).

HIP HOP CHIP SHOP

Inspired by the inventive and experimental ethos of hip-hop culture, this very untypical fish and chip shop trades from an award-winning boombox catering trailer and is the creation of Manchester duo Jonathan "Ozzie" Oswald and Luke Stocks, who set out to revolutionize the UK's favorite dish. "This quintessentially British meal is all too often trapped by tradition. We doff our caps to the culinary past and forge our own path, using the traditional chippy menu as a blueprint for our innovation – sampling culinary inspirations from around the globe. It's not a 'chippy tea' – it's a 'hip hop chip shop tea.'" Don't worry if you're feeling a bit lost – just tuck into their ultra-fresh Fish Rap, B.I.G. Fish Dogg (chunky strips of crispy North Sea coley goujons served on a homemade poppy seed hot dog bun) or their wickedly tasty Onion Blings and you won't care what it's called. To quote US rapper Immortal Technique: fish is good when that sh*t is fresh.

PORKY BY NATURE

Potato Scallops: • 4 Maris Piper potatoes • sunflower oil for deep frying • chili batter (see page 123)

Other ingredients: • mushy peas (see page 91) • sausage • bacon • gammon • sliced ham

Method: Potato Scallops. Wash and peel potatoes. Slice into ¾ inch (2cm) diameter slices. Wash slices in cold water till water runs clear (shows that all the starch is removed from the potatoes). Boil the slices till the potato is on the verge of breaking up and drain till all the water is removed. Place on a tray in the freezer for roughly 15 minutes, till the potatoes are cold. Preheat a deep fat fryer to 260°F (130°C). Place slices in fryer until golden brown, remove from heat and place on a tray back in the freezer till fridge-cold. Cling film and place in the fridge till the final preparation stage.

Final preparataion stage: Preheat the deep fat fryer to 375°F (190°C). Coat the potato scallops in flour and completely cover in the chili batter. Place in the fryer until the scallops are golden brown on both sides. Remove from fryer, drain off excess oil and place three slices on a plate. Add the hot minty peas to the top of the scallops equally covering all three slices. Coat your sausage, bacon, gammon, shards of ham with flour and cover in the original beer batter. Place into the fryer and cook until golden brown and drain any excess oil. Push the ham into the top of the mushy peas and serve. For a nice extra bit of crispy texture you can finely chop some shallots and sprinkle over the dish.

KASA INDIAN EATERY

The passionate team behind Kasa includes British-born, lawyer turned-chef Anamika Khanna and "business geek-turned-aspiring restaurateur" Tim Volkema. Ex-LSE Anamika has been cooking Indian food since she was a little girl growing up in London and India. She is driven by a desire to share her vision of Indian food with a broader audience. Tim's been feasting on Indian food his whole life and always believed it could be done better. After sampling Anamika's simple, home-style Indian food, he decided to leave his brand manager position at Kraft Foods, uproot his family and move out West to run the front of house operations at Kasa. Tim (MBA from Northwestern's Kellogg School) and Anamika first set up the successful brick-and-mortar Kasa in San Francisco. When in 2011 they learned that the Council would start taking applications for food truck permits, they camped outside the offices for three rainy nights, amongst other hopeful candidates looking for prime spots in the city. It wasn't plain sailing though, and after picking two great downtown locations for their as-yet unbuilt trucks, they were taken to court by enraged local sandwich-and-soup establishments and forced to try a different tack. A few years on and the truck has won out in San Francisco. Kasa is a much-loved local treasure serving original and different food to hungry workers and sightseers. They say, "we love what we do and we're proud and privileged to be a part of this community. We just want to make Indian food that would make our grandmothers proud!"

PINEAPPLE CHICKEN
serves: 4

- 1 pineapple, cored and cut into small cubes • 8 chicken drumsticks • 1 lemon or lime, juice squeezed • 3 tbsp soy sauce • 1 tbsp ginger, finely chopped • 1 tbsp garlic, finely chopped • 3 green chilies, finely chopped • ½ tsp red chili powder • 1 green bell pepper, chopped into large cubes • 1 onion, chopped into large cubes • 3 tbsp fenugreek leaves • 2 tbsp cumin seeds • salt to taste • 3 tbsp oil

Method: Heat oil in a deep pan. Add the cumin and fry until the seeds start to splutter. Now add the ginger, garlic and green chili and cook for 30 seconds. Add the chicken and cook over high heat until the juices seal. Season the chicken with the lemon juice, soy sauce, salt, red chili powder, and fenugreek seeds. Add the onions and bell peppers and fry for another minute over high heat. Cover and cook for 15-20 minutes until the meat is cooked through and tender.

Van Leeuwen

Van Leeuwen Artisan Ice Cream can be seen in trucks across New York City or Los Angeles, serving their delicious ice cream. Brothers Ben and Pete Van Leeuwen and Laura O'Neill first started with two ice cream scoop trucks in 2008. Asked what sets them apart, they say, "we celebrate ingredients perfected by nature, not science." Van Leeuwen make their ice cream from scratch in Greenpoint, Brooklyn, using only fresh hormone- and antibiotic-free milk and cream, cane sugar, egg yolks and the best fruits, chocolates, spices and nuts from small producers locally and around the world. They now have six trucks and three stores around Brooklyn and Manhattan; in 2014 they opened an Artisan Ice Cream Truck in Los Angeles. Taking the business to L.A. has meant no need to hibernate in winter months, and the fulfilment of a dream for the trio, who had always planned to head west. Their top tip? "Use cocoa butter where you can...it's awesome!"

VAN LEEUWEN STRAWBERRY ICE CREAM
Makes: about 1 quart (1 litre)

For the ice cream base: • 2 cups (475 ml) heavy cream • ½ cup (120 ml) whole milk • ¾ cup (150g) sugar • ¼ tsp kosher salt • 6 large egg yolks
For the strawberry compote: • 10 oz (285g) fresh or frozen strawberries, hulled and diced • ½ cup (50g) sugar • 1 tbsp fresh lemon juice

Method: To make base, pour cream and milk into a heatproof bowl set over a saucepan of gently simmering water. Whisk in ½ cup (100g) of the sugar and salt. Stir until both dissolved. Warm the mixture until steam rises from the top.

Meanwhile, prepare an ice bath in a large bowl and set another bowl over it.

In a medium bowl, whisk together egg yolks with the remaining sugar until uniform. While whisking, add a splash of hot dairy mixture to the yolks. Continue to add the dairy mixture, bit by bit, until you've added about half. Add the yolk mixture to the remaining dairy mixture in the double boiler. Set the heat to medium to medium-low, and cook the custard, stirring continuously, until steam begins to rise from the surface and the custard thickens enough to coat the back of the spoon; (hold spoon horizontally and run your finger through the custard. If the trail left stays separated, custard is ready to be cooled). Strain custard into bowl sitting over ice bath and stir for 3 to 5 minutes, or until custard has cooled. Transfer to a quart-size container, cover, and refrigerate for at least 4 hours or, preferably, overnight. While custard cools, in a non-reactive bowl, combine strawberries, sugar, and lemon juice and let stand for at least 2 hours. If necessary, cover and refrigerate until ready to use. Using a potato masher, mash the strawberries until the compote is chunky. Combine chilled custard with 1½ cups of strawberry compote. Stir until well mixed. Pour the custard into an ice cream maker and freeze. Churn ice cream until texture resembles "soft serve." Transfer to a chilled storage container and freeze until hardened to your desired consistency. You can serve it immediately (it will be the consistency of gelato). The ice cream will keep, frozen, for up to 7 days.

NORDIC STREET FOOD

Street food crusaders Pernilla Elmquist (Swedish Masterchef contestant 2011) and Jens Almgren opened their Malmö food truck a year ago to great success. A dream for many years, the plucky Pernilla says she wanted to start Nordic Street Food to improve the quality of local food truck nosh, using seasonal produce and to benefit local producers. "I had long wondered about street food... I wanted to have an option on the days I do not stand at the stove, or when I do not have the opportunity to go out to a restaurant." The pair decided to explore Scandinavian cuisine. Pernilla counts herself lucky to live in southern Sweden's rural Skåne and credits the landscape with influencing a lot of her foodie ideas. "The changing nature of the forest and lake outside my cabin gives me inspiration for new culinary challenges." Their menu reflects Nordic conditions and traditions, and changes regularly. You're likely to find venison (slow-cooked for 16 hours), horseradish cream, sour cabbage, sweet and sour lingonberry flatbreads, and a range of Swedish beverages like Birchwater and Äppelmust. As the proud owners of the world's only truck to serve new Nordic food (from a brand new Peugeot) they have attracted a lot of plaudits. The year after they opened they were runners up for Best Dish, Best Sandwich and they won Best Overseas Trader at the British Street Food Awards.

NORDIC CHANTERELLE WRAP
serves: 4

- 1lb 5 oz (600g) Swedish chantarelles • 3 ½ oz (100g) white cabbage • 1 red onion
- Westerhavs cheese (from Jylland, Denmark) • 4 tbsp white vinegar • parsley
- 3 ½ tsp (0.5 cl) ättika (Swedish vinegar) • 6 ½ tbsp of sugar • ¼ pint (0.1 l) water
- butter • sea salt • 4 pieces of Swedish flat bread (from Jämtland if possible!)
- 4 tbsp sour cream

Pickled onions: Peel and slice the onions in thin slices. Pour ättika, sugar and water in a pot and boil, so that the sugar melts. Add the sliced onions and let it cook for ten minutes on low heat. Let it cool.

Sour cabbage: Thinly slice the white cabbage and put it in a bowl. Pour vinegar over it and sprinkle salt on top. Leave it like that for half an hour. Chop parsley and mix it with the cabbage.

Chantarelles: Clean the chantarelles with a brush and let them slowly fry without butter a few minutes on medium heat, so that the water disappears. Add a big piece of butter, turn up the heat and fry the chantarellse for about a minute or two. Sprinkle sea salt over.

Heat the bread for a few seconds in a dry frying pan. Spread sour cream on the bread. Top with sour cabbage, fried chantarelles, grated cheese and pickled onions. Wrap and eat!

MILK TRUCK

The Milk Truck team first got their start at the indoor Brooklyn Flea in 2010, thrilling grilled cheese lovers with classic American sandwiches from their food stand. Owner Keith Klein says, "I'd been researching food trucks for a while and one morning around 5 a.m. I just woke up and thought, 'Grilled cheese.' It's simple, it's familiar and it hits you in the happy place." After expanding into other flea markets, they put their first truck on the road ("we call her Bessie") in 2012. Since then, they've licensed their menu to the folks at Houston Hall, started selling made-to-order mac & cheese from their Mac Bar (open Saturdays at Smorgasburg and rated #1 in the city by *Village Voice*), built a catering kitchen for their growing catering business and sponsored a Little League team. "We've been busy! But we still cut our bread by hand to get the right thickness for our bread slices. We still obsess about making sure that each ingredient is in a sandwich for one reason and one reason only: to make that sandwich delicious." And with grilled cheese sandwiches comprising aged gruyere, cultured butter and Balthazar Levian Pullman bread, it's clear that these are not just your average truck snacks. "Even though it's slower," says Keith, "we still make every sandwich to order, by hand. We really believe that if we make and serve delicious things, it will make people happy."

MILK TRUCK ALL DAY SANDWICH DELUXE
Serves: 4

• 8 slices of Balthazar rye batard bread • 8 oz (225g) sliced or grated gruyere • 4 x1 oz (30g) slices of applewood smoked ham • 4 fresh eggs • 1 medium yellow onion, sliced thinly • 4 oz (110g) mushrooms, sliced • ½ lemon • 2 oz (60g) clarified butter • olive oil • 4 sprigs of thyme, leaves only • 1 tbsp sugar • 1 tsp salt + more for seasoning if required • pepper

Method: Heat a large skillet over medium heat. Add 2 tbsp oil. Add onions and cook until softened. Add 1 tbsp sugar and a dash of salt, toss and continue to cook until onions are golden and slightly caramelized. Remove from pan and place on plate to cool. Heat a large skillet over medium heat. When hot, add a healthy glug of olive oil. Add the mushrooms and thyme. Sauté for a few minutes until browned. Salt to taste and remove from heat. Squeeze a bit of lemon juice over the mushrooms and set aside. Wipe out the skillet, replace on heat and add a fresh glug of olive oil. Gently break four eggs into the pan, season with salt and pepper. Let the whites set a bit, then break the yolk. Flip the eggs and cook for another 30 seconds. You want the yolks to be just a little runny. Remove from pan and hold. Heat a panini maker according to instructions, or a ridged, cast iron pan over medium heat. Butter the outside of eight slices of bread. On the unbuttered sides add gruyere, one slice ham, egg, a teaspoon of caramalized onions and a teaspoon of mushrooms. Cover with remaining bread slices so buttered sides face out. Place in panini grill (two at a time) until bread crisp and cheese melted. (If using cast iron pan, place smaller pan on top to weight sandwich down; turn after a couple of minutes.) Cut in half and serve hot!

The BEIGNET TRUCK

When Chris Bautista first tried deep-fried choux pastry fritters (a.k.a. beignets) at the New Orleans-style Jazz Kitchen in Disneyland he fell in love. Many years and many trips to New Orleans later, the result was The Beignet Truck, which first hit the streets of L.A. in 2013. "Our biggest challenge was finding the right, high-quality ingredients," says Chris. "We are dedicated to offering only the finest and freshest ingredients and coffees imported from New Orleans." This approach gives his dishes the edge when it comes to creating the right flavors, and the Beignet truck has as a result carved out a successful niche in L.A. with a straightforward menu of beignets, coffees and gourmet hot chocolates. His other secret? "An amazing team, as friendly as the folks back in New Orleans!"

THE BEIGNET TRUCK BEIGNETS

- ¾ cup room temperature water • ¼ cup granulated sugar • 1 ¼ tsp (or ½ an envelope) of yeast • 1 large egg • ½ cup (120 ml) of evaporated milk • ½ tsp salt
- 3¼ cups of bread flour • ¼ cup of shortening • cottonseed oil (amount depends on method of frying) • 1 cup sugar

Optional: ⅛ tsp nutmeg • ¼ tsp cinnamon • ⅛ tsp ground cloves

Method: In a mixing bowl, add water, sugar and yeast. Whisk together and let sit for 5-10 mins, or until all the yeast and sugar have dissolved and white bubbles begin to form. In a separate bowl, whisk together the egg, evaporated milk and salt. After yeast has been fully activated, add contents of both bowls into a larger mixing bowl and whisk. Add 1 ¼ cups of flour and, if you wish, additional spices including nutmeg, cinnamon and ground cloves (note: New Orleans beignets do not include spices).
Mix together to form a batter-like mixture. Add shortening and mix thoroughly.
Add remaining flour and mix with a wooden spoon. Once most of the flour has been mixed in, transfer dough to a hard, well-floured surface and knead until all the flour is mixed in. The dough should be very slightly sticky; if it is too moist, add more flour until it is easier to work with.
Place dough back into a bowl, cover with a clean towel, and let sit in a warm (80°F / 25°C is ideal) area for roughly 2 hours. The dough should double in size. Then place dough on a floured cutting board and begin rolling out with a rolling pin to around ½ inch (1 cm) thick. Then cut into any shape desired. (Note: square or rectangle shapes maximize the number of beignets.) Lightly flour each side. Place the cut beignets on a baking sheet, cover once again, and let rise for half an hour. Once beignets have re-risen, carefully place inside a deep fryer or pot with cottonseed oil set at 350°F (175°C). The beignets should sink, then float within a few seconds and immediately begin to puff up. Turn beignets about every 15 seconds until golden brown: 1½ - 2 minutes. Remove and let them rest on a bed of paper towels for 2 minutes. Dust with a generous helping of powdered sugar and enjoy!

Extras

Recipes from the World's Best Food Trucks

Cremas

BUSKRUID'S HORSERADISH CREAM

• fresh horseradish • crème fraîche • lemon • virgin olive oil
• sea salt & freshly ground black pepper

Method: I like preparing the horseradish cream a day before so all flavors have time to settle, but preparing it on the same day is just fine as well.

Put the crème fraîche into a big bowl and grate the fresh horseradish with a zester above it. The amount of horseradish depends on how strong you want the cream to be, you will have to try and see. With a spoon slowly mix in the juice of half a lemon, a splash of olive oil and season with salt and freshly ground black pepper.
Great with Red Beetroot Soup with Sweet Potato (see page 15).

DIE DOLLEN KNOLLEN'S SOURED CREAM

• 9 oz soft cheese • 2 oz whipped cream • 1 small onion, finely cut
• 2 oz fresh herbs (chives, parsley) • 1 clove garlic
• salt & freshly ground black pepper

Method: Mix all the ingredients and chill in the refrigerator for half an hour.
Serve with Potato Latkes (see page 63).

CINNAMON SNAIL'S SRICHACHA CREAM

• 1 scallion, minced • ½ cup vegenaise or other vegan mayonnaise alternative
• 2 tbsp sriracha sauce • 2 tbsp maple syrup

Method: Combine all ingredients in a small bowl, whisking for about 30 seconds, until an even orange color develops. Serve with Korean BBQ Tofu Tacos (see page 25).

CILANTRO CREMA

• 1 cup sour cream • ¼ cup fresh cilantro (coriander) leaves, finely chopped
• ½ lime, juiced • salt & freshly ground black pepper

Method: In a small mixing bowl, combine the sour cream, cilantro and lime juice.
Mix thoroughly; season with salt and pepper.

MEXICAN CREAM

• ½ cup Mexican sour cream • ½ tsp lime zest, finely grated • 2 tsp lime juice

Method: Combine all the ingredients and mix well. It can be stored in a covered container in the refrigerator for up to 2 days.

FAT SHALLOT'S REMOULADE SAUCE

- 1 cup homemade mayonnaise (see page 115) • 1 cup coarse grain mustard
- 5 cloves garlic, minced • 3 tbsp Louisiana hot sauce • 1 tsp kosher salt

Method: Whisk all ingredients together in a bowl. Tadum!
Serve with Pulled Pork Sandwich (page 27).

LUARDOS "SPECIAL" SAUCE

- 6 tbsp mayonnaise • 4 tbs yogurt • 1 tbs chipotles en adobo (or substitute for 1 tsp paprika) • 1 clove garlic, crushed • ½ lime, juice of • pinch of sea salt

Method: Mix all ingredients together in a bowl.

FISH DOG'S TARTARE SAUCE

- 2-3 tbs homemade (see page 115) or good quality mayonnaise
- 10-12 small gherkins, roughly chopped • 1tbs capers, rinsed and chopped
- a squeeze of lemon juice

Method: Mix all ingredients together in a bowl.

GIOVANNI'S SPICY TOMATO SAUCE

- 1 tin plum tomatoes • 3 cloves garlic • 1 whole fresh chili • 6-8 basil stalks
- olive oil • sea salt • black pepper

Chop garlic and fry gently in olive oil. Add some chopped basil stalks and a whole fresh chili. Pierce the chili with a knife so it doesn't explode when frying. Add plum tomatoes, lightly season with sea salt and freshly ground black pepper. Gently simmer for 30 minutes. Remove the chili.

BARBECUE SAUCE

- 1 tbsp olive oil • 1 onion, finely chopped • 400g can chopped tomatoes
- 3 garlic cloves, finely chopped • 85g brown sugar • 3 tbsp malt vinegar
- 2 tbsp Worcestershire sauce• 1 tbsp tomato purée

Method: Heat oil in a saucepan and add the onion. Cook over a gentle heat 4-5 mins, until softened. Add remaining ingredients, season and mix. Bring to the boil, then reduce heat and simmer for 20-30 mins, until thickened. For a smooth sauce, simply whizz the mixture in a food processor or with a hand blender for a few seconds.

Dressings

HORSERADISH DRESSING

• 4 egg yolks • 1 tbsp English mustard • 2 tbsp white wine vinegar
• 1½ tbsp rapeseed oil • 2 tbsp creamed horseradish

Method: To make the dressing, place the egg yolks in a bowl with the mustard and vinegar. Slowly pour in the oil while whisking. Once all the oil has been added, add the horseradish and season to taste. Store in the fridge until ready to use.

EL TACO'S CILANTRO PESTO

• 1 pot cilantro (coriander) • 2 tbsp pumpkin seeds, toasted • ½ chili • 1 cup olive oil
• salt & pepper • 1 lime, juice

Method: Mix all ingredients in a blender, add oil for desired consistency. Season with salt and pepper. A must-have with Sol battered soft shell crab (see page 31).

ENGINE'S WASABI MAYO

If you've got time on your hands, make the mayo from scratch (see below) - it always tastes better. But for the quick way add wasabi to regular mayo from a jar. Start with 1 tablespoon wasabi powder (NOT paste), and slowly add water (1 teaspoon at a time) to make a runny green sauce. Now add 1 cup of mayo and fold gently. DO NOT use a blender - it will split. Make this mayo as strong as you like.

HOMEMADE MAYONNAISE

• 1 tsp mild mustard • 1 egg yolk • 1⅓ fl oz (40ml) vegetable oil
• 1 tbsp white wine vinegar • juice of 1 lemon • salt and pepper

Method: Mix the mustard and egg yolk with a whisk. Add salt and pepper and then, whisking continuously, half the oil a little at a time until the mixture begins to thicken. Once you have added half the oil, whisk in the vinegar. Gradually add the remaining oil and continue whisking until your mayonnaise is thick and pale in colour.

Salsas

PINEAPPLE SALSA

• 1 ripe pineapple, well skinned, sliced thin, diced • 1 red capsicum, roasted, peeled, diced • 1 bird's eye chili, finely diced • 1 bunch cilantro (coriander), finely chopped • ¼ fresh lime, juice of • ¼ cup orange juice, fresh squeezed • 2 tbsp brown sugar • 1 tbsp chipotle powder • 1 pinch salt

Method: Combine the pineapple, capsicum, chili and cilantro. Whisk remaining ingredients and pour over the salsa, tossing to coat.

LUARDOS' PICO DE GALLO SALSA

• 1 large vine tomato, seeds removed, finely diced • ½ onion, finely diced • 1 lime, juice of • pinch of sea salt • ½ tsp caster sugar • drizzle of olive oil • 2 tbsp fresh cilantro (coriander), chopped

Method: Mix ingredients together in a bowl. Check the sweet/sour balance and adjust by adding more lime/sugar as necessary. Serve with Luardos' Fish Tacos (page 39).

MEXICAN TOMATO SALSA

• 4 large firm tomatoes, skinned and deseeded • 1 fresh green chili (the fat squat variety that isn't too fiery), halved and deseeded • ½ medium red onion, finely chopped • 2 tbsp fresh cilantro (coriander), chopped • 1 lime, juice of • salt & freshly milled black pepper

Method: Chop the tomatoes into approximately ¼ inch dice into a serving bowl. Next, chop the chili very finely before adding it to the tomatoes. Add the onion, cilantro and lime juice, and season with salt and pepper. Give everything a good mix, then cover and leave on one side for an hour before serving.

GUACAMOLE

• 1 large ripe tomato • 3 avocados • 1 large lime, juice of • handful cilantro (coriander), chopped (hold back some for garnish) • 1 small red onion, finely chopped • 1 chili, red or green, deseeded and finely chopped

Method: Use a large knife to pulverise the tomato to a pulp on a board, then tip into a bowl. Halve and stone the avocados and use a spoon to scoop out the flesh into the bowl with the tomato. Tip all the other ingredients into the bowl, then season with salt and pepper. Use a whisk to roughly mash everything together. Cover with cling film and chill until needed. Scatter with the remaining cilantro. Indispensible adjunct with all that is Mexican.

Slaws

EL TACO'S CITRUS MAYO SLAW

• I head cabbage, shedded • 7 oz (200g) onion • 3½ oz (100g) fennel oz • 3½ oz (100g) silverskin onions • ½ oz (15g) mint • I tbsp mayonnaise • 2 large limes, juice of • salt & pepper

Method: Shred the cabbage, fennel and silverskins and mint, mix with mayonnaise and lime juice. Salt and pepper to taste. Serve with Sol Battered Soft Shell Crab (see page 31).

GASTROPOD STUPID SLAW (STUPID GOOD)

• 2 heads red cabbage, shredded • 3 large carrots, julienne strips • ½ cup salt • ½ cup sugar • apple cider vinegar

Method: Toss cabbage and carrots in salt/sugar mixture and combine well. Pack the salted vegetables into an appropriate crock. Add enough vinegar to completely submerge the vegetables. Allow to sit out at room temperature overnight. Refrigerate for up to I month.

THE FAT SHALLOT'S SLAW

• I head red cabbage, shredded • I head Napa cabbage, shredded • I carrot, peeled and shredded • I red onion, thinly sliced • 2 bunches dill, chopped • ¼ lb (115g) bacon fried till crispy, fat reserved • 2 tbsp coarse grain mustard • 3 cloves garlic, minced • ⅓ cup cider vinegar • ¼ cup olive oil • 2 tbsp kosher salt

Method: Combine all the dressing ingredients in a large bowl, add the shredded vegetables and coat well in the dressing. Let marinate for at least 2 hours, tossing every 30 minutes. When ready to serve mix in chopped bacon.

LA POPOTE'S COLESLAW

• I oz (30g) white cabbage • ½ oz (15g) grated carrot • I tsp mild mustard • I egg yolk • 1⅓ fl oz (40ml) vegetable oil • juice of lemon • Xérès vinegar • chives • salt • pepper • sugar

Method: First prepapre the mayonnaise. Mix the mustard and egg yolk. Add salt and pepper, and then the oil little by little until the mayonnaise begins to thicken. Add a few drops of lemon. Finely chop the white cabbage, grate the carrots, add the chopped chives and then mix in the mayonnaise. Add a few more drops of lemon juice and vinegar, a pinch of sugar, salt and pepper, and mix.

Spicy Relishes

THE GOOD LIFE'S JD ONION RELISH

• 4 large onions • 3 garlic cloves, chopped • 2 tbsp Evoo • 4 tbsp brown sugar • 2 tbsp Italian herbs • 1 can tomatoes, diced • ½ cup BBQ sauce • salt • 2 shots Jack Daniels

Method: Heat Evoo in skillet on medium heat, add onions and fry until translucent. Add brown sugar and stir until it dissolves. Add garlic, mixed herbs, tomatoes – simmer for 4 minutes. Add BBQ sauce and Jack Daniels. Simmer for another 10 minutes and season with salt to taste.

CRISPY ONIONS

These more'ish morsels add a bit of crunch to your dish.

• 1 large onion • 2 cups of flour • 1 tbsp salt • 1 tsp paprika • pinch of cayenne pepper • rapeseed oil

Method: Combine dry ingredients in a bowl. Coarsely dice onion and coat in the flour mixture. Heat rapeseed oil (canola) in a deep pan to 375°F (190°C and fry the onions in batches for roughly 1 minute or until golden-brown. Drain on paper towels.

THE FAT SHALLOT'S JALAPEÑOS

• 10 jalapeños sliced very thinly • 1 cup cider vinegar • 1 tbsp kosher salt • ¼ cup sugar

Method: Place sliced jalapeños in a bowl. Place remaining ingredients in a pot and bring just to a simmer. Let cool and pour over jalapeños. Let sit over night or at least 12 hours.

SPICY TOMATO RELISH

• 1 tbsp olive oil • 2 tsp ground cumin • 1 bay leaf • 2 garlic cloves, crushed • 2 small shallots, chopped • 1 red chili, chopped • 1 celery stick, chopped • 1 lb 2 oz (500g) very ripe tomatoes, roughly chopped

Method: Heat oil in a large frying pan and add the cumin. Let it cook for a moment, then add the bay, garlic, shallots and chili. Cook for 2 mins until soft but not colored, then add the celery and tomatoes. Sweat everything down gently for 20-30 minutes. Remove from the heat, season and leave to cool.

This can be made a few days in advance and kept in the fridge.

PEANUT CRUMBLE

In a mortar and pestle, crush the peanuts, or finely chop them with your knife. Combine the peanuts and brown sugar; set aside until ready to serve.

Breads, batters and more

CHILI PHILOSOPHER CORNBREAD
• 8 ⅛ oz (230g) all purpose flour • 4 ½ oz (130g) sugar • 2 tsp Salt
• 2 tbsp baking powder • 12 oz (350g) cornmeal • 1 ½ pts (750ml) milk • 4 eggs
• 13 ½ oz (380g) melted butter • 3 ½ oz (100g) sweetcorn

Method: Preheat the oven to 400°F (200°C) gas mark 6.
Line a 9x5in (23x13cm) loaf tin (pan) with baking parchment and grease. Sift the flour into a mixing bowl and add sugar, salt and baking powder and cornmeal. Stir to blend. In a separate bowl whisk eggs and milk together. Add the dry ingredients to the eggs and milk. Stir until just blended; do not over mix. Finally add the melted butter (or lard if you prefer) to the batter and pour into the tin. Bake until a skewer inserted into the centre comes out clean, about 45 minutes. Serve hot or at room temperature.

EMPANADA DOUGH
makes: 20 empanadas.

Dough: • 1lb 2oz (600g) flour • 2 oz (50g) butter, melted • 6 tbsp olive oil
• 1½ cups (350 ml) water • 1 tsp salt

Method: Sift flour, dig a well and add the remaining ingredients. Add water until you obtain a compact ball. Let stand at least 1 hour in the refrigerator. Flour the work surface. Roll out the dough. Cut discs 8 inches (20 cm) in diameter.

CRÈPE BATTER
• 5 oz (150g) flour • 6 fl oz (175 ml) milk • 5 fl oz (150 ml) water • 1 large egg, cage-free

Method: Heat canola oil in a deep pot or fat-fryer. Whisk flour, milk, water and egg together till mix is thick but not goopy.

LUARDOS' BATTER MIX
For the batter: • 1 bottle Corona beer • 1 tsp paprika • 10 ½ oz (300g) plain flour
• large pinch sea salt

Method: Whisk the ingredients together. The batter should be the consistency of American pancake batter.

BATTER / CHILI BATTER.
• 1 can of cheap lager • 2 tbsp of baking powder • 1 whole lemon • 4 tsp table salt
• 12 oz (350g) of plain flour • splash of malt vinegar
(for chili batter add 2 tsp chili powder and 4 tsp chili flakes)

Method: Put the flour in a mixing bowl. Add baking powder, the juice of one whole lemon, vinegar and salt to flour. Slowly add a can of lager whilst whisking till it becomes a batter-like paste. Dip a spoon into the mixture, lift out and make a figure of eight motion over the mixture. When the batter is ready the figure of eight will be continuous without stopping at any point.

Weights & Measures

WEIGHTS			DIMENSIONS			VOLUME	
Imperial	Metric		Imperial	Metric		Imperial	Metric
½ oz	10 g		⅛ inch	3 mm		2 fl oz	55 ml
¾ oz	20 g		¼ inch	5 mm		3 fl oz	75 ml
1 oz	25 g		½ inch	1 cm		5 fl oz	150 ml
1½ oz	40 g		¾ inch	2 cm		(¼ pint)	
2 oz	50 g		1 inch	2.5 cm		10 fl oz	275 ml
2½ oz	60 g		1¼ inch	3 cm		(½ pint)	
3 oz	75 g		1½ inch	4 cm		1 pint	570 ml
4 oz	110 g		1¾ inch	4.5 cm		1¼ pint	725 ml
4½ oz	125 g		2 inch	5 cm		1¾ pint	1 litre
5 oz	150 g		2½ inch	6 cm		2 pint	1.2 litre
6 oz	175 g		3 inch	7.5 cm		2½ pint	1.5 litre
7 oz	200 g		3½ inch	9 cm		4 pint	2.25 litres
8 oz	225 g		4 inch	10 cm			
9 oz	250 g		5 inch	13 cm			
10 oz	275 g		5¼ inch	13.5 cm			
12 oz	350 g		6 inch	15 cm			
1 lb	450 g		6½ inch	16 cm			
1 lb 8 oz	700 g		7 inch	18 cm			
2 lb	900 g		7½ inch	19 cm			
3 lb	1.35 kg		8 inch	20 cm			
			9 inch	23 cm			
			9½ inch	24 cm			
			10 inch	25.5 cm			
			11 inch	28 cm			
			12 inch	30 cm			

Note: All these are approximate conversions, which have either been rounded up or down. In a few recipes, it has been necessary to modify them very slightly. Never mix metric and imperial measures in one recipe; stick to one system or the other.

All spoon measurements on this site are level, unless specified otherwise.

Cup conversions

AMERICAN CUP CONVERSIONS

American	Imperial	Metric
1 cup flour	5oz	150g
1 cup caster/ granulated sugar	8oz	225g
1 cup brown sugar	6oz	175g
1 cup butter/margarine/lard	8oz	225g
1 cup sultanas/raisins	7oz	200g
1 cup currants	5oz	150g
1 cup ground almonds	4oz	110g
1 cup golden syrup	12oz	350g
1 cup uncooked rice	7oz	200g
1 cup grated cheese	4oz	110g
1 stick butter	4oz	110g

LIQUID CONVERSIONS

American	Imperial	Metric
1 tbsp	½ fl oz	15 ml
⅛ cup	1 fl oz	30 ml
¼ cup	2 fl oz	60 ml
½ cup	4 fl oz	120 ml
1 cup	8 fl oz	240 ml
1 pint	16 fl oz	480 ml

Note: A pint isn't always a pint: in British, Australian and often Canadian recipes you'll see an imperial pint listed as 20 fluid ounces. American and some Canadian recipes use the the American pint measurement, which is 16 fluid ounces. Our recipes use the American measure.

The US/UK/Canadian Gallon: The gallon is a measure of volume approximately equal to four liters. Historically it has had many different definitions, but there are three definitions in current use. In United States customary units there are the liquid ($\approx$ 3.79 l) and the lesser used dry ($\approx$ 4.4 l) gallons. There is also the imperial gallon ($\approx$ 4.55 L) which is in unofficial use within the United Kingdom and Ireland and is in semi-official use within Canada. The gallon, be it the imperial or US gallon, is sometimes found in other English-speaking countries.

OVEN TEMPERATURES

Gas Mark	°F	°C
1	275°F	140°C
2	300°F	150°C
3	325°F	170°C
4	350°F	180°C
5	375°F	190°C
6	400°F	200°C
7	425°F	220°C
8	450°F	230°C
9	475°F	240°C

Contact Details / Truck Index

Credits

Front Cover – © Ian Castello-Cortes; p.4 – Jon Darsky & his mobile pizzeria Del Popolo, photo by Matthew Millman, matthewmillman.com; p.6 – photo by Megan Mack, meganmack.com, courtesy of Natasha Case, Coolhaus; p.10 – photo by Reid Yokoyama, reidyokoyama.com; p.16 - photo by Jimmy Thornton – Eat A Duck food blog, eataduck.com/; p.17 – recipe courtesy of Coolhaus, from the *Coolhaus Ice Cream Book*, © 2014 by Natasha Case & Freya Estreller with Kathleen Squires, published by Houghton Mifflin Harcourt, New York 2014; p.20 – photo by Michelle Edmunds, MichelleEdmundsPhotography.com; p.22 – photo by Peter Fristedt, flickr.com/photos/fristedt; p.29 – photo by Robert Yager, facebook.com/RobertHYager; p.34 – photo by Phillip Pessar, phillippessar.tumblr.com; p.38 – photo by ©Toby_Allen, tobyallenphotography.co.uk; p.50 – photo by Thanh Lai, wonthanhphotography.com; p.54 – photo by The Gaztronome, thegaztronome.com; p.56 – photo courtesy of Ms P's Electrick Cock; p.61 – Fresh Rootz shack built by Digby Platt, Stone Monkey Yoga Studios, photo by Claudia Vye, claudiavye.com; p.62 – photo by Florian Böhm, florianboehm.com; p.64 – photo by Nina Strassgütl, ninastrg.de; p.70 – photo by Lynn Chyi, lynnchyi.com; p.74 – photo by Flavor Please, flavorplease.com (with thanks to Ian Serlin); p.86 – photo by Emma Cochrane; p.88 – photo by Charlie Whatley, charliewhatley.com; p.89 – recipe courtesy of The Bowler, from *The Bowler's Meatball Cookbook* by Jez Felwick, published by Mitchell Beazley, London 2013; p.95 – photo by Brian McGarvey; p.102 – photo by Sidney Bensimon, sidneybensimon.com; p.110 – photo courtesy of Chingón; p.112 – photo courtesy of Fritèz; p.116 – photo courtesy of Carb & Nation; p.118 – photo courtesy of Chingón; p.116 – photo courtesy of El Taco Truck; p.122 – photo courtesy of The Chili Philosopher.

Acknowledgements

The publisher would like to thank all the brilliant food trucks, with their talented chefs, who took part in this project; Coolhaus' Natasha Case for her insightful introduction; Ian Serlin from Flavor Please for his invaluable advice and assistance on US food trucks; Richard and Jess from Engine for their good-humor during the shooting of the cover; Love and Scandal coffee shop in London SE1, for putting up with a lot of camera equipment during the shoot. Most of all we'd like to thank the food truck movement for reinvigorating our taste buds. We can't go without also thanking the Citroën motor company, for creating that perfect work of motorized art: the Citroën H van.

Food Truckin' Volume 2

There were so many trucks that we wanted to include in this book, but sadly we didn't have the space. However we have arrived at a simple solution: **Food Truckin' 2 (a.k.a. Keep on Food Truckin')**. If you know of a food truck – from anywhere in the world – whose delicious food you feel should get a wider audience, write to us at contact@graffitobooks.com. We aim to reply to all emails within 24 hours. Thanks and we look forward to hearing from you!

The editors at Graffito Books, London

Front cover image: The Engine food truck in London, with Jess at the wheel and Richard in the kitchen.
Back cover images, clockwise from top left: Kogi truck from L.A.; Chingón from Melbourne, Australia; Dub Pies from NYC; The Good Life from Cape Town, South Africa; La Popote from St Tropez, France; Frankie's Coffee from Stockholm, Sweden.

Index by Cuisine

A note on cilantro (coriander)

We don't know whether there is a song about this, but the word 'coriander' means different things on different sides of the pond. Listen carefully as this could get confusing. Americans and Canadians call cilantro (fresh coriander), quite rightly, 'cilantro'. The English, however, call cilantro 'coriander'. 'Coriander' in the US and Canada refers, of course, to cilantro seeds. The English also call cilantro seeds 'coriander'. If you're talking to an English woman, or an Englishman, you'll never know whether they mean cilantro or coriander. We blame 1588, and the failure of the Spanish Armada's invasion attempt on England. One serious effect of this was to deny the English a rich Spanish heritage in their cultural mix and, by extension, the English never discovered the word 'cilantro'. We have tried to be fair to both sides of the pond. Where you see 'coriander' in brackets after 'cillantro' – as in cilantro (coriander) – it's to keep the English happy. We don't mean that you can use either cilantro or cilantro seeds. We mean use cilantro!